POCKET PIKETTY

POCKET PIKETTY

JESPER ROINE

OR Books
New York · London

© 2017 Jesper Roine

Published by OR Books, New York and London
Visit our website at www.orbooks.com

All rights information: rights@orbooks.com

First printing 2017

Cataloging-in-Publication data is available from the Library of Congress.
A catalog record for this book is available from the British Library.

ISBN 978-1-68219-068-5 paperback
ISBN 978-1-68219-069-2 e-book

Text design by Under|Over. Typeset by AarkMany Media, Chennai,
India. Printed by BookMobile in the United States and CPI Books Ltd
in the United Kingdom.

CONTENTS

PREFACE

This book was originally written in Swedish in the spring of 2014, just after the English-language publication of Thomas Piketty's *Capital in the Twenty-First Century*. In Sweden, as in the United States and in many other countries, Piketty's book caused massive debate. Having worked on top income inequality, and being familiar with the book and the underlying research, I participated in this debate mainly by trying to correct views and statements that I thought were based on misunderstandings of what the book actually said. I also tried to provide background to the research underlying Piketty's book to explain why it was such an important achievement and to elucidate the different, often conflicting positions put forward by different commentators. Having noticed my activity, two friends suggested I put all this together into a short book, to give an introduction to all of those for whom the original text was too much. The idea was to make at least the basic facts and reasoning accessible to as many people as possible. The result was basically the book you are reading now.

Even if the discussions surrounding Thomas Piketty's book have calmed down and disappeared from the main headlines, they are by no means over. On the contrary: his work has given rise to a great number of research projects delving deeper into to different parts of his arguments. This work is ongoing and constantly evolving and will continue for a long time.

Had I been asked to introduce and summarize the book today, it is possible that I would have emphasized some things more, and others less, but essentially I think the introduction and the summary would not be much affected by the time that has passed. The final concluding part would perhaps have lengthened, due to the many additional topics that have been raised since the spring of 2014. Its main conclusions would remain unchanged.

Would I have written this book if asked today? I hope so. The original motivation—to make it possible for as many people as possible to appreciate the importance of *Capital in the Twenty-First Century* and participate in the discussions it started—is still present. If anything, this feels even more important today than two years ago.

— Jesper Roine
Stockholm, October 2016

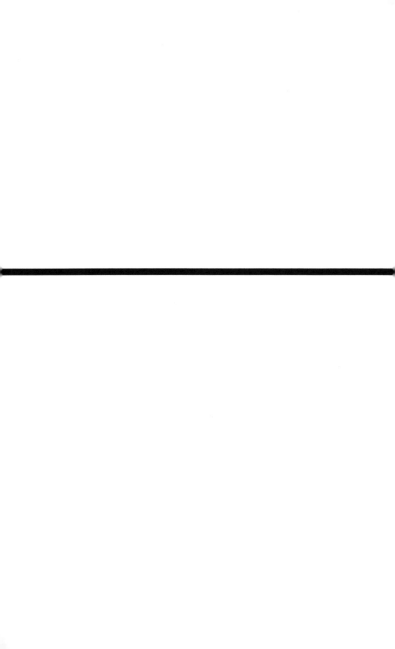

I

THE UNDERLYING
RESEARCH

WHY ALL THE FUSS?

In spring 2014, Thomas Piketty's book *Capital in the Twenty-First Century* burst onto the world stage. It was suddenly everywhere, topping various bestseller lists and prompting reactions from all sorts of people, from Nobel laureates and other prominent academics to social commentators from different camps. Opinion remains divided. Some see the book as a watershed that fundamentally changes our understanding of how the economy works, while others challenge the premise of the book and question the data provided.

Personally, I found all the fuss a little surprising. The book first appeared in French back in 2013, and much of the book is based on research Thomas Piketty and others have been working on for over a decade. Many of the results concerning the historical trend of income and wealth flows have long been there for anyone to find.

As for my own background, I have been part of the research network that has spent the past decade or so identifying long-run historical series for income and wealth distribution in a host of countries. Together with Daniel Waldenström at Uppsala University, I produced the Swedish series for top income shares over the twentieth century as found in the World Top Income Database, which forms an important source in Piketty's book. Daniel and I also created a series for Swedish wealth concentration since the nineteenth century. Together with a number of colleagues (Anders Björklund, Henry Ohlsson and Jonas Vlachos) in various constellations, we wrote about specifically Swedish issues concerning income and wealth distribution and drew a range of international comparisons. Over the years, Daniel and I also published a number of articles on ekonomistas.se about this research.

On closer consideration, the attention *Capital in the Twenty-First Century* received is both understandable and deserved. Thomas Piketty's book is much more than a list of historical facts. It is an attempt, against a background of *historical facts*, to understand the underlying correlations and, based on this under-standing, to consider what can be done about growing inequality in society. In a time when many international organizations such as the OECD and the International Monetary Fund are expressing concern about the trend and President Barack Obama called inequality "the defining challenge of our time," it is hardly surprising a book claiming to explain how we got here and what should be done in the future has attracted such interest.

WHY THIS BOOK?

Does capitalism have a natural tendency to reinforce differences in people's income and wealth? Or is it perhaps the other way around—initial differences become smaller as the economy develops? Perhaps this phenomenon has varied between societies, and over time. To what extent does the answer depend on the way the economy is organized? How do these economic relationships relate to our views on fairness and meritocracy?

Classic theories from Ricardo to Marx to Kuznets have all dealt with this broad subject: the relationship between economic growth and the distribution of the gains from this development within the population. This is also the focus of Thomas Piketty's book *Capital in the Twenty-First Century*. The big difference is, in contrast to its predecessors, Piketty's book is not just a theory about how the economy works, but a theory based on facts about income and wealth distribution over the entire twentieth century, and on the relationship between capital and income all the way back to the eighteenth century. The reason Thomas Piketty was the first to formulate a theory on the basis of such facts is that our knowledge of these conditions is largely new. Much of this new knowledge has come out of research to which Thomas Piketty devoted himself over the past fifteen years.

Increased knowledge does not automatically mean the theory presented by Thomas Piketty in his book must be true. As with all theories, his was based on assumptions open to debate and challenge. It is also possible that, like so many of his predecessors, he was wrong in his predictions about the future—something he repeatedly emphasizes in the book. This does not make *Capital in the Twenty-First Century* any less important and it certainly does not diminish his research contributions. We now know more about key relationships in the economy, and in particular much more about income and wealth distribution over time, than we did a decade ago, and much of this is thanks to Thomas Piketty.

This new knowledge also creates a whole new platform for the debate on core issues for the future: What will happen to income and wealth distribution? Is it evident the modern economy automatically guarantees a meritocratic and democratic social order? How should we react if, for example, technological advances and globalization result in enormous returns but mainly for a small share of the population. What roles do policy and redistribution have to play in future developments and how do these affect inequality? Piketty does not answer all these questions, and objections can be raised to the answers he did provide, but as Harvard economics professor Larry Summers put it in a comment on Piketty's book: "Books that represent the last word on a topic are important. Books that represent one of the first words are even more important."

• • •

This work is divided into three parts. The first part gives a background by summarizing some of the research on which Thomas Piketty's book *Capital in the Twenty-First Century* was based. All the figures in this section have been created using data from the World Top Income Database (WTID), available online. The second (central) part is an attempt to summarize the book itself. The figures and tables in this part are all based on data available on Thomas Piketty's homepage and each corresponds to graphs and tables in Piketty's book. Finally, the third part is a short commentary on some of the issues debated just after the publication of *Capital in the Twenty-First Century*, as well as some points about the importance of inequality research in general. Common to all three sections is the obvious fact that I am responsible for any errors, and above all for any misinterpretations of what Thomas Piketty has written. The parts differ, however, in that the first and last part contain my own view of the underlying research and debate surrounding Piketty's book, while the second part is an attempt to summarize the content of the book objectively, free from any objections or reservations I might have.

• • •

A summary would not be a summary if it included everything that appears in the text being summarized. This is particularly relevant here since, despite being 685 pages long (970 if you read the French original), much of Piketty's book could already be described as a summary of the extensive research literature. To give a sense of proportion, Piketty's book on top incomes in France from 1901–1998, which contributed only a small part of the factual substance in *Capital in the Twenty-First Century*, runs to 807 pages. The two volumes on top incomes in twenty-two countries compiled by Anthony Atkinson and Thomas Piketty, which formed the basis for three of the book's sixteen chapters, are 604 and 776 pages long. With this in mind, it need hardly be said a summary of *Capital in the Twenty-First Century* can never be a substitute for reading the whole work in full.

Not only will a summary not contain all the details, but in this case it also deprives the reader of a terrific read. The focus of a summary tends to be on covering the key definitions and logical arguments with anecdotes, illustrative examples, and other digressions usually being omitted. That remains the case in this summary. This is usually no great loss when it comes to great tomes on the economy or economic history. *Capital in the Twenty-First Century* is, however, the clear exception that proves the rule, since it is extremely readable.

My hope is this summary and its attempt to draw out the key points will encourage more people to read Piketty's book in full, and to discuss the many important issues it raises.

THE UNDERLYING RESEARCH

In the 1950s, economist Simon Kuznets created the first long-run income inequality series ever produced. His time series covered developments in the United States over the years 1913–1948. He began with 1913 because that year saw the introduction of the modern income tax system in the United States, which generated an excellent source of information on individual incomes. Initially, only a small proportion of the population paid taxes— those with the highest incomes—but more and more people were included over the years. Since the share of the population covered in the statistics changed over time, Kuznets could not simply calculate the distribution among those who pay tax—doing so would say nothing about the overall distribution, nor would it be comparable over time. Instead, he combined data from the tax statistics with data from national accounts or other sources relating to total personal incomes in society. By defining a fixed fraction of the population (which necessarily comprised the top of the distribution, since they were the ones paying tax) such as the top one percent or the top ten percent, he was able to relate their income to the total. By calculating the share of total personal income earned by top income groups, he then created comparable estimates of income inequality over time.

Kuznets work and his explanations for what he observed—including the famous Kuznets curve (explained below)—attracted considerable interest and had a major influence on subsequent research. Kuznets was awarded the Nobel Prize for Economics in 1971 (coincidentally the year Thomas Piketty and I were born) in part for his research on economic growth and inequality.

For various reasons, Kuznets series were never updated in any systematic way. Instead, the focus was on gathering data that revealed the trend across the *whole* population, not just the top group. Other facts about individuals also began to be included in the analysis such as work, education, and family status. This made it possible to better explain why income was distributed the way it was—how it related to education, for example. It also allowed for more detailed studies of actual living conditions among the population. Comparability of data between countries also improved over time through projects such as the Luxembourg Income Study (LIS), which has put a great deal of effort into establishing comparability between countries that have different definitions of income and different rules on how it is taxed. For decades now, this type of data has been the main source for studies of income distribution.

This development was, of course, good in many ways since it enabled the study of issues that previously went unaddressed. Researchers gained a whole new way of identifying the reasons behind the income differences that occurred. It also enabled a meaningful discourse to begin about welfare and the most disadvantaged people in society. But it also had two clear downsides. Firstly, it meant the long-term perspective largely disappeared. In most cases, it was impossible to go any further back than the 1960s, and in many cases the time span was even shorter. Secondly, the sample surveys that formed the basis of the data were not designed to capture the very top of the distribution. If a relatively small random sample of the population happens to include an extremely rich person, their income or wealth (and changes to their income or wealth) will affect the picture of the overall distribution in a way that is far from representative. For this reason, very high levels of income and wealth are often excluded or *top coded*, meaning the person is simply recorded as having more than a certain amount.

It was against this backdrop of scarce historical time series and a lack of knowledge about the trend in the top of the distribution that Thomas Piketty in the late 1990s started his research aiming to create long-run income inequality series. The first fruits of this labor were published in 2001 in the almost one thousand-page book *Les Hauts revenus en France au 20e siècle: inégalités et redistribution, 1901–1998* ("High incomes in France in the twentieth century: inequalities and redistribution, 1901–1998"), which launched the research program that continues to this day. Shortly after, in 2003, came a corresponding study of the trend in the United States for the years 1913–1998 in an article by Piketty and his colleague

Emmanuel Saez. At the same time, Anthony Atkinson studied the trend in the United Kingdom and also encouraged many other researchers to do the same in their own countries. Over the course of just a few years, studies appeared in a large number of countries, with researchers applying the same methods and concepts in order to make the data as comparable as possible.

The result of all this research was, to use Piketty's words, to "extend and generalize what Kuznets did in the early 1950s—except that we now have fifty more years of data, and over twenty countries instead of one." The material now includes the top income shares (and a whole host of related details) for twenty-seven countries, collated and readily available in the World Top Income Database. The renewed interest in historical income distribution trends has also helped spark greater interest in the history of long-run wealth distribution, the development of inheritance flows over time, and the historical relationship between capital and income. Piketty has been a leading researcher in all these areas and, individually or with various co-authors, he is responsible for many of the key contributions made in the field.

THE DISTRIBUTION OF INCOME OVER THE TWENTIETH CENTURY

In the introduction to *Capital in the Twenty-First Century*, Piketty puts forward three areas of research as the empirical basis for the book. The main area relates to *income distribution over time* and, as described briefly above, the second is *wealth distribution over time*. The third is about the *relationship between capital and income over time*. The explicit aim of the first two is to give a picture of the *distribution among individuals* while the third addresses *the relationship between two totals* (capital and income), but says nothing in itself about their respective distribution. If, however, one combines information from the distribution of income and wealth (from the first two areas of research), it is possible to make assumptions about how the change in the ratio between capital and income, for example, affects distribution of income among individuals. The time perspective for each research area has consistently been centuries rather than years or decades.

In my view, one could also add another area, looking at *the size of inheritance flows in relation to the rest of the economy over time.* The results of this research form the basis for Chapter 11 of *Capital in the Twenty-First Century* and also implicitly underpin some of the book's normative discussion.

Below I describe a few key results from one of these three (or four) research areas: income inequality over the twentieth century.

TOP INCOME SHARES OVER THE TWENTIETH CENTURY

Out of the research areas that form the empirical foundation of Thomas Piketty's book, the most developed is that concerned with what we know about income distribution over time. Since the most common method has been to follow Kuznets example from the 1950s and combine tax statistics with national accounts, the data are limited by the point at which a country introduces systematic annual taxation of individual incomes. For most of the countries studied, this takes place in the early twentieth century. In Sweden, our first observations date from 1903, while in some countries it is possible to go even further back in time (to the late nineteenth century in Norway, Germany, and Japan, for example). For other countries, the series begins later (e.g., 1932 in Argentina, 1947 in Singapore, and 1986 in China).

There have naturally been many changes over time in terms of how income is defined, who pays tax (individuals or households), how great the problem of tax avoidance and evasion may have been, and so on. Such matters differ between countries, and taking account of such differences has been a major and time-consuming challenge within this research. In practice, the approach has largely been to examine how the tax system has changed, and then to calculate what impact different assumptions and potential errors in the data might have on the final series. The aim has always been to calculate how great a proportion of all income—that is the sum of wages, capital income, and business income—that goes to different groups at the top of the income distribution (before tax and transfers), and to do this in a way that provides as accurate a picture as possible.

A key aspect of these series, and of most other measures of income distribution, is they give a snapshot for a particular year, a new picture for the next year, and so on, without taking account of *who* is at the top. Our interpretation of income inequality will, of course, be very different depending on whether the same people come out on top year after year or the distribution shows signs of considerable mobility. In short: are the high earners the same individuals over time, or do people climb up and down the income ladder? Several studies have attempted to answer this question, and the general result is that the trends we see in the repeated cross-sections broadly capture changes in the distribution of individual income rather than changes in mobility.

For those who wish to delve more deeply into how the series for each country have been produced and the details concerning how sensitive the various series are to all sorts of considerations, the results are published in two books (each as thick as *Capital in the Twenty-First Century*): *Top Incomes in the Twentieth Century* (2007) and *Top Incomes—A Global Perspective* (2010), both edited by Anthony B. Atkinson and Thomas Piketty.

The data used in these publications are available online in the World Top Income Database; http://www.wid.world which is constantly updated with new data.

FOUR KEY INSIGHTS

What has this research shown? Let us start by looking at the overall trend. Figure 1 shows the development of the income share for the ten percent of the population with the highest incomes in a number of countries—let us call this group the "top 10 percent." The lines indicating the development have been faded for most countries so as to highlight what has happened in three of them: the United States, France and Sweden. These three are broadly representative for the overall trends in Anglo-Saxon countries, Continental Europe and Scandinavia respectively. The clutter of lines where individual countries are almost impossible to distinguish shows a surprisingly common trend up until around 1980. The share of all income earned by the top decile of the population—the top ten percent—falls, on average across a large number of countries, from just over forty percent in the early twentieth century to a little under thirty percent. In some cases, such as Sweden, the drop is even

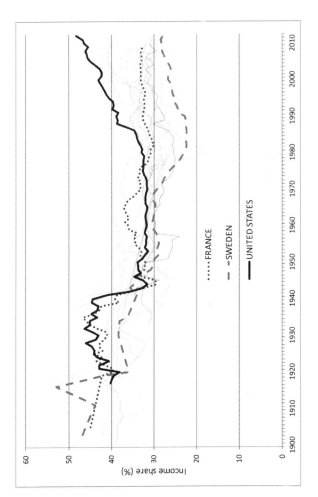

Figure 1. The top ten percent's share of income over the twentieth century

more pronounced—from around fifty percent to just over twenty percent. But since about 1980 there is more divergence. The income share for the top ten percent has increased on average, but in some countries, such as the United States, the increase has been pronounced, and in others such as France much less so.

If we now separate out the trend *within* the top ten percent, an at once interesting and previously largely unknown aspect of the trend manifests itself. In Figures 2 and 3, the trend in the top ten percent is split in two: the income share for a top one percent group (referred to at times as P99–100, which stands for percentile ninety-nine to percentile one hundred and thus relates to those people in the top one percent) and the rest of the top ten percent (which can correspondingly be called P90–99). If we first consider the trend for the top one percent, their income share falls from around twenty percent of all income in the early twentieth century, to a little over five percent around 1980. This is a large drop and accounts for much of the whole decrease in the top ten percent group. Similarly, much of the top decile's upswing in recent decades derives

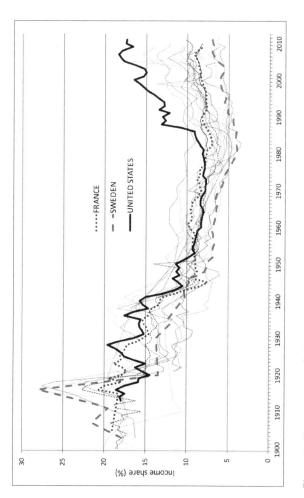

Figure 2. Top one percent's share of income 1860–2012

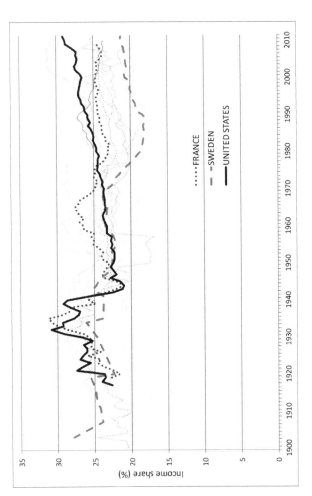

Figure 3. Top ten percent's share of income minus top one percent's share

from an increase in the top one percent. This is confirmed when we look at the trend for the rest of the top decile (P90–99), whose income share on average stood at around twenty-five percent throughout the twentieth century. In other words, fluctuations in the top one percent account for much of what happened to the income share for the top ten percent during the twentieth century, while surprisingly little happened to the rest of those at the top.

Another interesting and previously overlooked detail can be found in the timing of the fall that occurred in the first half of the twentieth century. The diagram below, focusing on France and the United States, clearly shows much of the decline for the top one percent coincides with the Great Depression of the 1930s and the two world wars. One might even go so far as to say that if we take out the downturns during the war and depression, nothing happens to the top one percent's share of income during the first half of the twentieth century.

The contrast between the United States and France also provides a third insight concerning the trend over more recent decades. These countries can be said to represent developments since the years around 1980 in a number of Anglo-Saxon and Continental European nations. In the former, the income share for top earners has increased significantly, particularly in the United States, where the income share for the top one percent is almost back to the levels of the early twentieth century. This American U-shape for the twentieth century has garnered a great deal of attention and lies behind the expression that we are living in a "New Gilded Age," which refers back to the period around the turn of the previous century, when enormous private fortunes were built up in the United States. Continental Europe—represented by the French development in the diagram— has also seen the top income shares rise since around 1980, but to a much lesser extent.

A fourth insight from this work concerns the composition of income, i.e., proportion of income from labor and proportion of capital income. Figure 4 below shows how much of the income earned by the top one percent derives from capital from the 1920s onwards. Capital share increases in the 1920s and then declines

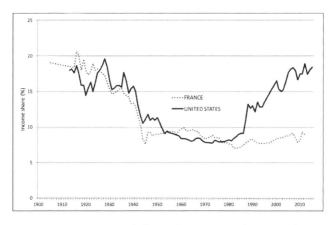

Figure 4. Top one percent's share of income over the twentieth century in France and United States

sharply in the United States during the depression and in both the United States and France during the Second World War. These latter falls are so large they alone explain practically the whole decline in the top ten percent's income share.

When it comes to the trend of recent decades, the diagram also shows the strong upturn in the United States is *not* due to increased capital income in the top group.

On the contrary, seen over recent decades this has fallen somewhat in the United States, while increasing slightly in France (where the top group's income share has only risen marginally). This shows that the steep rise in the top share of income in the United States is due to considerable rises in salary for those who earn the most, rather than increased capital income.

Together, the new series give us at least four new insights into developments over the past one hundred

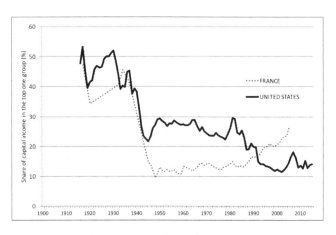

Figure 5. Capital income as a share of top one percent's income over the twentieth century in France and United States

years: 1) much of the change in the income share of the top ten percent is driven by changes in the top one percent; 2) much of the decline that took place in the twentieth century is (at least in certain countries) driven by specific shocks which in turn affect capital income; 3) in recent decades, top income shares have risen dramatically in certain countries (the United States), while others have seen much more modest increases (France); and 4) where the rise is greatest, it is driven primarily by wage income rather than capital income. These insights are important to bear in mind as we move on.

WHY DOES THIS MATTER?

And so to the big question: What of all of this is new, and how does it affect the way we see our society today? There are many possible answers to this question, but one way to answer it is to go back to the 1950s and Simon Kuznets results and his tentative attempt at an explanation—the famed Kuznets curve.

Kuznets studied developments during the first half of the twentieth century. His series gave a picture of the trend in the United States, and to this he added preliminary results from certain other countries. His overall conclusion was the top income shares had fallen sharply since the First World War. This surprised Kuznets, since he saw several reasons why the concentration of income would rather be expected to grow. Against this background, he formulated an idea that was able to accommodate his new insights. His approach was to imagine an economy that modernizes through the rise of a new sector—in Kuznets case the industrial sector.

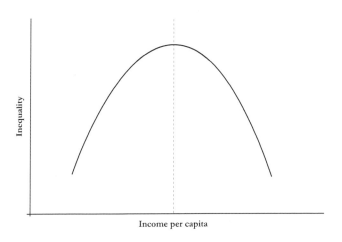

Figure 6. The Kuznets curve

Productivity in this new sector is higher than in the traditional sector—agriculture. Early on in its development, only a small portion of the population works in the new, more productive sector, with the result income inequality initially rises. This was something Kuznets thought might have happened in the nineteenth century. But as more and more people enter the new sector and are able to share in the fruits of its higher productivity, income inequality gradually shrinks over time, something that matches the trend he observed.

According to this optimistic view, income inequalities would thus follow a progression in which they would first increase and then reduce as the whole of society benefitted from the higher productivity in the modern sector. Such a progression can be presented graphically as an inverted U—a Kuznets curve.

A summary of the new research, however, indicates Kuznets explanation if taken literally was incorrect. For one thing, the general idea that income inequalities reduce as economic development progresses does not hold. Over the past 30–40 years, top income shares (and most other measures of income inequality) have risen in the majority of countries and systematic studies of the relationship between income inequality and economic development have suggested the general trend does not exist. There is simply no evidence economic growth has any general link with reduced income inequality over time. The trend over the twentieth century has in fact been U-shaped, rather than following the inverted U of Kuznets theory.

But Piketty's series tell us much more than that. They show developments during the first half of the twentieth century were almost entirely driven by a fall in the income share of the top one percent and this in turn was almost entirely due to a decline in capital income. If we look at the top share of all *wage income*, instead of the sum of all income sources, it remains relatively constant during the first half of the twentieth century. Adding the studies of wealth concentration during this period confirms the role played by capital in explaining the decline: The top one percent in the wealth distribution see their share of all wealth approximately halve over the period, with substantial falls during the world wars and the Great Depression.

All this combines to suggest the main explanation for the major change we see in income distribution over the first half of the twentieth century has little to do with Kuznets idea that productivity increases in the modern sector would automatically benefit everyone. The differences in wages between the top and the rest of the distribution are marginal compared with the impact of a steep fall in capital income at the top. Above all, it shows there is no automatic mechanism that reduces inequalities in pace with development.

The new, more detailed, series on development also show how wrong we can go if we treat the top ten percent as a single entity. The group actually proves to comprise very different people in terms of income composition and development. To understand the trend, we therefore need to study both changes *within* the top group, as well as changes in capital income and labor income.

TECHNOLOGY, EDUCATION, AND THE POSSIBILITY OF A NEW KUZNETS CURVE AFTER 1980?

These insights—the importance of studying the composition of income and also distribution within the top group—are crucial in that they give a new picture of what took place in the first half of the twentieth century, but also because they are important in understanding the increased concentration of income in recent decades.

One possible explanation for the growing income inequalities since around 1980, which in many ways goes back to Kuznets idea, lies in technological progress and education. In simple terms, one might imagine that technological changes, for example in the IT sector, create increased demand for highly skilled workers. If the education system keeps pace with the technological progress, with the supply of highly skilled people growing at the same speed as demand for such people, this has little effect on their wages relative to the less well educated. However, if technology makes rapid progress and the supply of skilled labor is unable to keep up, this increases competition for skilled workers and their wages go up. In this scenario, wage inequality can be understood in terms of *A Race between Technology and Education,* which is also the title of a terrific book by Claudia Goldin and Larry Katz that aims to explain the trend in United States wage inequality over the twentieth century.

These ideas and developments on the theme of *skill-biased technological change* (which in these studies often equates to "technological progress that favors the well educated") have had a major impact on research in recent decades. A large number of studies have also been published showing these ideas can explain aspects of the trend over time. However, the new income distribution series also highlights a few key problems.

Firstly, it is striking how much of the income growth is driven by the very top (the top one percent, or even the top 0.1 percent). If education was the determining factor behind the growing inequalities, we would observe a much broader upswing across the whole upper part of the distribution, rather than the current situation, which shows a strong rise at the very top and much smaller changes among those who have relatively high wages, but are not among the very top earners. Given this development, we have to seek out explanations for how a small number of people, who are admittedly often well educated, have come to earn so much more of the total in recent decades (there are many such explanations, which are often lumped together under the title "*superstar* theories").

Secondly, it once again proves important to look at the trend for the different types of income – is it income from labor or capital? As illustrated above, much of the development in the United States is driven by increased wage inequality, while the relatively small upturn seen in France is explained more by a return to the significance of capital income.

All in all, this again illustrates the importance of considering developments at the top alongside the composition of total incomes, in order to gain an accurate picture of the trend.

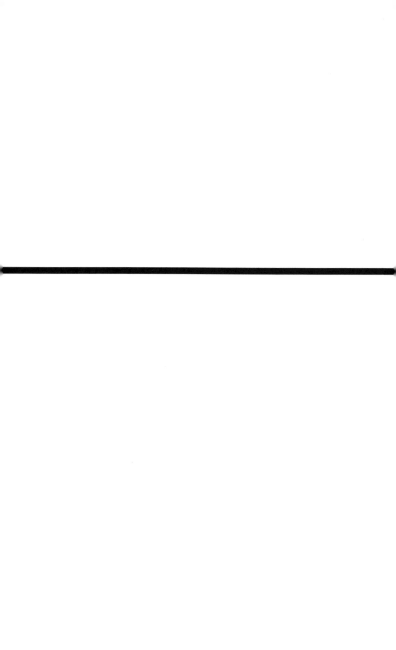

II

SUMMARY OF *CAPITAL IN THE TWENTY-FIRST CENTURY*

STRUCTURE OF THE BOOK

In addition to an introduction and a short concluding summary, *Capital in the Twenty-First Century* comprises sixteen chapters, split into four sections, plus almost a hundred pages of endnotes, references, digressions and clarifications. Piketty also published an extensive technical appendix online in which he explained and expanded on his arguments. The first part, *Income and Capital*, introduced a few basic concepts and relationships that then reoccur throughout the book. This first part is split into two chapters. Chapter 1 defines concepts such as gross domestic product, national income, capital and the basic ratio of capital to income. The chapter also introduces an important formula called the *first fundamental law of capitalism*. This expresses how capital's share of national income can be described as the product of the rate of return on capital and the capital/income ratio. This relationship is neither controversial nor surprising, but rather an accounting identity. It is nevertheless a relationship that proves useful in illustrating several later points. The second chapter presents nothing less than the broad history of the global economy, in terms of economic growth and demographic change over the past two thousand years, with a particular focus on developments since the Industrial Revolution. The purpose of all this is to provide some background to the rest of the book.

The second part of the book, *The Dynamics of the Capital/Income Ratio,* then outlines what we know about the aggregate relationship between the capital stock and the flow of income over time. This part explains how the nature of capital has changed since the eighteenth century in terms, for example, of the relative size of its components, such as agricultural land, housing, and other domestic capital. It also discusses the effect of state expansion on the relationship between public and private capital, and the role that international capital flows have played. Part Two is comprised of four chapters (3–6). In terms of empirical analysis, the different chapters have a slightly different geographical and temporal focus. Chapter 3 presents what we know about the growth of the capital stock and its relation to income in France and the United Kingdom since the eighteenth century. These are the countries for which we have most detailed historical data. Chapter 4 examines similar trends in Germany and the United States, but over a slightly shorter time period. Chapters 5 and 6 then expand the horizon to include other countries for which we only have data from the latter part of the twentieth century to the present day.

In Chapters 5 and 6, Piketty also presents a theoretical framework he thinks useful for understanding what we observe in the data. In Chapter 5 he introduces the *second fundamental law of capitalism*, which relates savings and economic growth to the level of the capital/income ratio over time. In contrast to the first "law," which is an identity, the second formula only holds in the long run and under certain, but general, circumstances. Underlying the *second fundamental law* is a standard abstraction of the economy in which production takes place through combining capital (in a broad sense) with labor. These so called factors of production then in some way share the value of what is produced in the form of return on capital and labor income. Some of the value is consumed, while some is saved and contributes to the future capital stock. Over time—decades rather than years—and *for a given amount of saving and a given rate of growth*, this process leads to a particular ratio between capital and income in the economy given by the so-called second fundamental law. The relationship says nothing, however, about what form the savings take, who saves, or why. It also says nothing about what drives the growth or why it reaches a given level. In reality it might of course be the case that growth changes with savings or vice versa. If, for example, the capital stock is very large and growth small, it is likely that savings would fall rather than remaining constant. Nonetheless, Piketty believes the formula is useful in understanding why the capital/income ratio has changed the way it has. In Chapter 6, this new-found understanding of the development of the capital/income ratio is linked to the effect such development has on capital's share of national income.

Part Three of the book (Chapters 7–12) then moves from the aggregate relationships to the *distribution of capital and income among individuals* in society. The focus here is on what we know about income and wealth distribution, how it has developed and also on the significance of wealth as a source of income for certain groups and how that has changed over time. In addition, Piketty showed why it is so important not just to look at the overall distribution, but also to follow changes within the top of the distribution and also why it is important to distinguish between different sources of income. The presentation of all these facts is followed by a discussion of how best to understand the long-running inequality trends based on the book's most central relationship—that between the return on capital, r, and the rate of growth in the economy, g. Based on data over the very long run Piketty noted that, with the exception of most of the twentieth century, the return on capital, r, has been larger than the economic growth rate, g, that is $r > g$. This implies that wealth accumulated in the past grows faster than output and wages. Chapter 11 explains how the inheritance flow has changed in relation to national income over time in France (the only country studied in detail so far, although projects are ongoing in Sweden and the United Kingdom) and how this development can largely be understood in terms of changes in the capital/income ratio. Finally, Chapter 12 discusses how global wealth may develop over the coming decades, and also how the fact that the return on large fortunes appears to be greater than the average return may be an additional factor in reinforcing the effect of the inequality represented by $r > g$.

In contrast to the earlier parts, the fourth and final part of the book (Chapters 13–16) does not focus on data and historical trends, but is instead an outline of what Thomas Piketty sees as possible policy measures. He begins with a brief overview (Chapter 13) of how taxation, redistribution and pension systems developed in the twentieth century, before moving on to discuss progressive income tax (Chapter 14), the possibility of a global tax on capital (Chapter 15), and what approach should be taken with regard to public debt and the accumulation of public capital.

INTRODUCTION

The starting point for the book *Capital in the Twenty-First Century* is the assertion that the distribution of wealth is one of today's most widely discussed and controversial issues. But, asks Piketty, what do we actually know about the distribution of capital over the long run? Will the accumulation of private capital inevitably lead to a concentration of wealth among the few, as Karl Marx believed in the nineteenth century? Or might it be that the balancing forces of growth, competition, and technological progress lead to harmonization and greater equality, as Simon Kuznets believed in the twentieth century? What conclusions can we draw from the knowledge and the data to which we now have access?

The aim of the book is to try to answer these questions although the answers are bound to be imperfect and incomplete. Nevertheless, they have to be taken seriously, since they are based on a much larger set of historical and comparative data than was available to researchers of previous generations—data that stretch across three centuries and cover more than 20 countries. This represents a major improvement on what was possible in the past, when much of the discussion was, as he puts it, a debate without data.

The introduction mainly consists of a summary of the key results in the book. Since this text is in itself a summary, it may seem superfluous to spend time on summarizing the summary. It is, however, interesting to see which of the many conclusions can be drawn from the book Thomas Piketty chose to focus on.

First, according to Piketty, we should be cautious about applying a deterministic approach to economics when looking at the distribution of wealth and income. Historically, economic distribution in society has always had a political dimension and cannot simply be reduced to economic mechanisms. For example, the levelling out of income inequalities as seen in many of the countries studied in 1910–1950 was largely a consequence of the two world wars, and of political decisions taken in connection to these. Piketty also thinks the rising inequalities seen in most countries since around

1980 are also attributable to political decisions, primarily deregulation of the financial sector and changes in taxation.

The second conclusion, which Piketty presents as the most significant, is that there are powerful mechanisms in the economy which, under certain circumstances, tend to increase inequality over time. There are, of course, forces that act in the opposite direction, but Piketty believes that these alone are insufficient to balance a future increase in inequality.

The core mechanisms that promote increased *equality* are the diffusion of knowledge and investments in education. These are key both to productivity growth and to reducing inequality, within countries as well as between countries. In addition to education and diffusion of knowledge, there are other potential mechanisms that could reduce inequality, although Piketty sees these as theoretical possibilities rather than anything discernible from the data. One such idea is that as workers acquire knowledge and skills, they also increase their share of total income. Piketty calls such a development the *rising human capital hypothesis*, where economic rationality automatically gives rise to democratic rationality and a more equal society—in line with Kuznets thinking. Another optimistic belief is the idea that, in modern societies with greater life expectancy, we will increasingly work when young and then live off saved capital in older age. The tension between labor and capital is thus less divisive, since we all begin young and become old and therefore (on average) have an equal interest in both labor and capital. Piketty asserts both these optimistic scenarios are possible and to some extent correct, but that their influence is much less than one might think. There are few signs of the workforce seeing an increased share in national income over an extended period of time. "Nonhuman" capital appears almost as indispensible in the twenty-first century as it was three hundred years ago (even if, as we will see, its form has radically changed), and there is nothing to suggest that the trend will not endure. In addition, as has always been the case, the inequalities in wealth distribution occur primarily *within* age groups, with inherited money continuing to play an important (and possibly growing) role.

So what are the forces that increase inequality over time? Piketty highlights two issues. First, there appears to be a tendency (particularly in certain countries) for those with the very highest labor income to pull away from others, which leads to labor income being concentrated in the hands of fewer people. Secondly, and more importantly according to Piketty, there are processes related to the way in which capital accumulates over time that, in a world where return on capital, r, is higher than the growth in the economy, g, result in increasing inequality over time. The basic inequality represented by $r > g$ lies at the heart of the book and can thus be said to encapsulate the logic of Piketty's argument. When the return on capital is higher than economic growth (which has been the case throughout history, and is likely to be the case in the future), accumulated capital increases more quickly than income. Someone with inherited wealth only needs to save a fraction of the income from this capital for its size to grow more quickly than the economy as a whole. Under such conditions, it is, according to Piketty, almost inevitable that inheritance will dominate what a person can generate through work over his or her lifetime and the concentration of wealth in society will become much higher—potentially reaching a level incompatible with meritocratic values and social justice.

PART ONE:
INCOME AND CAPITAL

On August 16, 2012, thirty-four striking workers were killed by police during an ongoing dispute at a platinum mine in Marikana, South Africa. The conflict mainly concerned wages. The miners were demanding a doubling of their pay—from the equivalent of around five hundred euros to one thousand euros per month. Following the tragic events, the mining company agreed a pay raise of seventy-five euros per month.

This dramatic account begins the first part of the book. The story is told as a reminder, not only of the similarities between this incident and historical events, such as the shootings at the demonstrations in Haymarket Square in Chicago on May 1, 1886, or in Fourmies in northern France on May 1, 1891, but also of the fundamental question of how income from production is to be shared between labor and capital. This issue, and in particular the historical trend concerning capital's share of production, is addressed in Part Two of the book.

But to understand exactly what is meant by terms such as *production*, *national income*, *capital* and *wealth*, these terms need to be defined and their relations explained. This is the main purpose of Part One.

The economy can, in its most abstract form, be described as a process where value is created by combining capital and labor. This value is then shared between the owners of the capital and the workers in different proportions—as profit and wages.

This means that everything we produce in the world forms the basis for our total income. In global terms, all production in a given time period (often taken to be a year) is by definition equal to all income. This income can then in turn either be consumed or saved, and what is saved becomes part of the capital in the next period in one way or another. The relationship between production and income is in a way trivial, but also important. It means that in a given year, the world's total income cannot exceed the value of everything we have produced. Conversely, the value of everything we have produced must go to someone in the form of remuneration for work or capital that is somehow used in the process. It is worth emphasizing that the meaning of the term *income*, as used here, is rather broader than the common usage. Naturally, it includes pay, but also other forms of remuneration for work, and also every conceivable form of return for capital owners in the form of profits, dividends, interest, royalties and so on.

When looking at developments in individual countries, however, equivalence between production and income may not apply, since some of what is produced in one place may be owned by people in other countries. Perhaps the most familiar concept for measuring economic activity is *gross domestic product* (GDP). GDP is the value of all goods and services produced in a country over the period of one year. Since Piketty focused more on the distribution of income than on production, it makes more sense to focus on a different term—*national income* (NI). This is closely related to GDP, but does not represent the same thing. National income is calculated by taking GDP and deducting capital depreciation, i.e., the loss in value that occurs when the capital is used (or simply ages). That gives what is called *net domestic product* (NDP), which in practice tends to be around 90 percent of GDP. Finally comes the addition of income from production abroad that is owned by individuals in the country (or the deduction of income paid abroad, depending on the circumstances). The size of these flows varies, but in most cases the net flow tends to be quite small.

In summary, we have the following definition:

National income = net domestic product + net foreign income

This income naturally goes to someone, and in turn can therefore be split into two main components:

National income = capital income + labor income

In short, the total income comes to us in the form of remuneration for work and as income for those who own capital.

But what does capital actually mean? Piketty defined it as everything that can be owned and traded on a market. As such, capital includes *natural capital*, such as land and natural resources (to the extent that these can be owned and exchanged on a market) and *produced capital*, which includes *physical capital*, such as buildings, machinery and infrastructure, *financial capital*, such as cash, shares and bonds, and also *intellectual capital*, such as patents. In certain societies and historical periods, this has also included people in the form of slaves. It is, however, important to note that it does not, in Piketty's book, include what economists often call *human capital*. This is, according to Piketty, an unfortunate term which should be included as part of an individual's labor (page 46 in *Capital*). In practice, different forms of capital naturally generate different forms of returns, and it can sometimes seem as if certain capital generates no income at all. But Piketty makes no such distinction. Since capital is everything that can be owned and exchanged on some market, it follows that all forms of capital can be transformed from one type to another and can therefore be seen as a single entity.

In the same way as all income in the economy goes to someone, everything defined as capital is also owned by someone. This means that capital and wealth can be seen as synonyms. The total wealth in society may, however, be owned either by private individuals or by the state. This means that national wealth can be divided up into private wealth and public wealth. As with income, wealth located in a country can also be owned by people in that country or elsewhere. These insights allow us to define the following relationships:

National wealth = private wealth + public wealth

and

National wealth = national capital = domestic capital + net foreign capital

Armed with a clearer understanding of the terms income and capital (or wealth, which in this context is the same thing), we can now define how the economy operates in terms of these two abstractions. In the economy, we essentially produce what we value by combining labor with our capital. This activity creates an *income flow*, which we measure over a given time period as, for example, GDP per person per year, or national income per year. Capital, on the other hand, is not a flow. Instead, it comprises the current value of everything we have accumulated over time. It grows through us saving part of what we produce, while at same time falling in value through depreciation or destruction.

An intuitive way to give a sense of the size of the capital stock (*K*)—the total value of all capital in society—is to relate it to the annual income flow (*Y*). This ratio, which recurs throughout the book, is called the *capital/income ratio* (β). To give a concrete example: if a country's capital stock is equal to the sum of the country's national income over six years, then $\beta = 6$ (or $\beta = 600\%$).

Using this ratio, it is now simple to express capital as a share of national income. This share, represented by β, is determined via what the book refers to as the *first fundamental law of capitalism*. This is really just a definition, but an important one that also reoccurs throughout the book. The "law" expresses capital's share of national income (α) as the product of the return on capital (*r*) and the ratio (β) of capital (*K*) to income (*Y*). That is:

$$\alpha = r \times K/Y = r \times \beta$$

This means, to take the example given in the book, if the capital stock amounts to six years of national income flow, i.e., $\beta = 600\%$, and the return on capital is five percent, capital's share of national income is $\alpha = r \times \beta = 5\% \times 600\% = 30\%$.

The evolution of the capital/income ratio across countries and over time, and its effect on capital's share of income via the *first fundamental law of capitalism*, are the focus of Chapters 3–6 in Part Two. But first, Chapter 2 provides an overview of the world's economic and demographic development over the past two hundred years (and to some extent, the past two thousand years).

Although Chapter 2 is not about introducing concepts and defining relationships, it presents background information that proves important in understanding the discussions running through the rest of the book. The focus is on understanding what a major effect small differences in annual growth rates have on development over time, and how long periods with three to four percent economic growth are exceptional compared with periods of one to two percent growth.

This is illustrated quite starkly in Table 1 below (Table 2.2 in Piketty), which shows the effect that different levels of annual growth have when applied, year after year, over a long period. If the economy grows by 0.1 percent per year, which was the long-term growth globally before the Industrial Revolution, the economy grows by three percent in one generation (thirty years), making it 1.03 times larger than it was at the outset. If this pace continues for one hundred years, the economy will become eleven percent larger and over one thousand years, the economy will become 2.72 times larger than it was in the beginning. If the population grows at the same rate, which was the long-term trend globally before the Industrial Revolution, average economic living standards remain constant. If, on the other hand, the economy grows by 1.5 percent per year, it will become over fifty percent larger in just one generation, and over a hundred year period will have grown to almost 4.5 times its original size. The table clearly illustrates how enormous differences arise from relatively small annual variations when applied over the long term, something that is important to bear in mind when considering what is a reasonable growth rate for the future.

This is important because part of Piketty's argument rests on how realistic—or rather unrealistic—it is

Table 1. The law of cumulative growth

An annual growth rate equal to …	… is equivalent to a generational growth rate (30 years) of …	… i.e., a multiplication by a coefficient equal to …	… and multiplication after 100 years by a coefficient equal to …	… and a multiplication after 1,000 years by a coefficient equal to …
0,1 %	3 %	1,03	1,11	2,72
0,2 %	6 %	1,06	1,22	7,37
0,5 %	16 %	1,16	1,65	147
1,0 %	35 %	1,35	2,70	20,959
1,5 %	56 %	1,56	4,43	2,924,437
2,0 %	81 %	1,81	7,24	398,264,652
2,5 %	110 %	2,10	11,8	52,949,930,179
3,5 %	181 %	2,81	31,2	…
5,0 %	332 %	4,32	131,5	…

future economic growth will be higher or lower than we might be accustomed to. The point is not, of course, to predict what is going to happen, but simply to illustrate lower growth is not unrealistic and it is important to consider what will happen in that scenario.

One key detail here is the economic growth used to support the argument is the economy's *total* growth, i.e. the *sum of demographic growth and productivity growth*. In many cases, we are concerned with growth per person. Population increases typically increase total production but do not, of course, automatically increase production *per person*. However, if we are interested in the size of the total economy, then demographic growth makes a difference. To illustrate the significance of this: globally, over the past one thousand years, mean production per person has risen by a factor of thirteen or so. On average, we thus produce thirteen times more "value" per person today than we did one thousand years ago. At the same time, the world's population has risen by a factor of about twenty-two. This makes the total size of the economy $13 \times 22 = 286$ times larger than a millennium ago.

Table 2 (Table 2.1 in *Capital*) illustrates how this growth breaks down into changes in output—overall and per person—and demographic growth over different historical periods.

The table shows how practically everything that has happened in growth terms has taken place in the last three hundred years and most of it is concentrated in the last hundred years. Average growth does, of course, conceal the major variations in economic development between countries. Table 3 (Table 2.5 in *Capital*) illustrates per capita output growth between continents.

Table 2. World growth since the Industrial Revolution (average annual growth rate)

Years	World output (%)	World population (%)	Per capita output (%)
0-1700	0.1	0.1	0.0
1700-2012	1.6	0.8	0.8
1700-1820	0.5	0.4	0.1
1820-1913	1.5	0.6	0.9
1913-2012	3.0	1.4	1.6

Averaged out, the differences look fairly minor, but the effect over the past two hundred years since the Industrial Revolution has been enormous. If an average country in Africa with a growth rate of 0.7 percent per year had started at the same level as an average European

Table 3. Per capita output growth since the Industrial Revolution (average annual growth)

Years	Per capita world output (%)	Europe (%)	America (%)	Africa (%)	Asia (%)
0-1700	0.0	0.0	0.0	0.0	0.0
1700-2012	0.8	1.0	1.1	0.5	0.7
1700-1820	0.1	0.1	0.4	0.0	0.0
1820-1913	0.9	1.0	1.5	1.1	2.0
1913-2012	1.6	1.9	1.5	1.1	2.0
1913-1950	0.9	0.9	1.4	0.9	0.2
1950-1970	2.8	3.8	1.9	2.1	3.5
1970-1990	1.3	1.9	1.6	0.3	2.1
1990-2012	2.1	1.9	1.5	1.4	3.8
1950-1980	2.5	3.4	2.0	1.8	3.2
1980-2012	1.7	1.8	1.3	0.8	3.1

country, which grew by an average of 1.5 percent over the past two hundred years, income in the African country would have risen by a factor of four, while income in the European country would be up by a factor of twenty.

None of these figures should be taken as precise, since measuring this type of growth throws up a whole host of issues. Nevertheless, two things stand out. Firstly, the average long-term growth rate, even in the most successful countries, has not been higher than one to 1.5 percent. The instances where the long-term growth rate has stood at three to four percent (or in some cases more) relate to economies that lagged a long way behind and have been able to quickly catch up with the others. Secondly, a growth rate as low as one or 1.5 percent leads to major changes in a society over a long period. In just one generation (thirty years) annual growth of one percent leads to a cumulative increase of more than thirty-five percent. If the growth rate is 1.5 percent, that increase becomes over fifty percent. To put this in concrete terms, the growth rate in Europe, North America and Japan has historically hovered around this level and it is abundantly clear how their societies have changed over this period.

PART TWO:
THE DYNAMICS OF THE
CAPITAL/INCOME RATIO

While the first part of *Capital in the Twenty-First Century* introduces concepts such as income and capital, and describes the world's economic development in broad terms such as economic and demographic development, the focus of Part Two is on how the capital/income ratio has developed and what effect this has had on capital in relation to total income.

Part Two of the book opens by presenting the trend in Britain and France since the eighteenth century. These countries have the most detailed historical data and can therefore provide the clearest picture of the trend over the long run. Detailed historical information on wealth and its importance for individuals comes in forms other than pure statistics, however. Piketty also illustrated several points with reference to the novels of Honoré de Balzac and Jane Austen.

The way in which wealth is discussed in the novels clearly shows how aware the readers of the time must have been about the importance of property, and how much was required in order to live on the income from it. Capital appears to be a constant presence and almost always takes one of two forms: land or interest-bearing government bonds. From this perspective, it can seem as if today's capital is entirely different and more "dynamic." Piketty points out, however, that although almost all capital took these forms, this does not automatically mean that all ownership was passive. Some characters, such as John Dashwood in Jane Austen's *Sense and Sensibility*, live purely off an inheritance. But many of Balzac's figures create their own fortunes. Père Goriot makes his fortune as a pasta maker and grain merchant. By selling his successful company and investing in interest-bearing government bonds, he is able to help his daughters enter Parisian high society. Even on his deathbed, abandoned by his daughters, he still dreams of lucrative investments. Another Balzac character, César Birotteau, makes his fortune in the perfume industry but, in contrast to Goriot, he loses everything in a failed attempt to increase his wealth through real estate speculation.

What are the differences between the nineteenth century and today? If he were living today, would Père Goriot have been a Steve Jobs? Have there actually been any deep changes when comparing nineteenth century capital and the wealth of today? Both then and now, there appears to be a combination of passive and active capital. Some fortunes are created, others inherited, some grow and others are lost—but is the sum of the whole actually so different from two hundred years ago? If not, how is it that most of us still have a sense that wealth and its distribution is somehow not the same as it was in the nineteenth century?

To begin answering these questions, Piketty studied the development of the capital/income ratio in Britain and France in the years 1700–2010. He also studied the composition of the capital stock over this period. From this he drew two clear conclusions. Firstly, he notes that the capital/income ratio, β, has developed in almost the same way in both countries. Over the whole period from 1700 to the early twentieth century, β remains relatively constant at 6 to 7 hundred percent, i.e., the value of the capital stock equals between six and seven times the national income. This level is almost the same in Britain and France. Over the first half of the twentieth century, this changed dramatically. During the First World War, the capital/income ratio fell sharply and then continued to decline during the Great Depression of the 1930s and the Second World War. Around 1950, the relationship between capital stock and income flow reached its lowest level historically at two to three hundred percent. Thereafter, the capital stock has slowly recovered and is now back at a level of around five to six hundred percent.

Once again, these figures are not exact, but the general trend is clear: a consistently high level over more than two hundred years, a steep decline in the first half of the twentieth century, then a gradual recovery to almost the same level as before the decline. In relation to national income, capital is now almost at nineteenth century levels. The brief explanation for this development is that the wars and crises of the first half of the twentieth century reduced the capital stock, so that to some extent by the mid twentieth century there was the impression that "capitalism had been structurally transformed," as Piketty puts it.

This development is both dramatic and important, but at the same time the similarity with today's levels conceals significant changes in the composition of the capital since the nineteenth century. In short: although its value in relation to national income is the same today as it was a century ago, it is now comprised of entirely different things. This is the second clear conclusion that Piketty drew. In very broad terms, the change in the structure of capital involves agricultural land losing importance and being replaced by housing and other forms of domestic capital (mainly business and financial capital invested in firms and government organizations).

This change is hardly surprising since, in the eighteenth century, agriculture accounted for two thirds of the countries' economies, both in terms of production and employment, compared with just a few percent today.

Figures 7 and 8 (Figures 3.1. and 3.2. in Piketty), illustrate these two main conclusions for Britain and France in the years 1700–2010. One detail worth noting is the role that foreign capital played in the late nineteenth century, when colonial possessions were at their height, and how it then fell away in the first half of the twentieth century. It is a significant component, but by no means the greatest source of change.

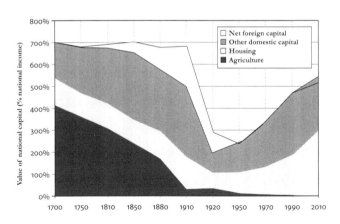

Figure 7. Capital in Britain, 1700–2010

The fourth chapter illustrates the trend in Germany and the United States, countries for which there are also historical series for the past few centuries. The German trend proves to be strikingly similar to that of France and Britain in the late nineteenth century (we are unable to trace the trend further back than that). The level of the capital/income ratio before the First World War stands at six hundred to seven hundred percent, just as in Britain and France. It then falls to between two hundred and three hundred percent around 1950 before slowly recovering.

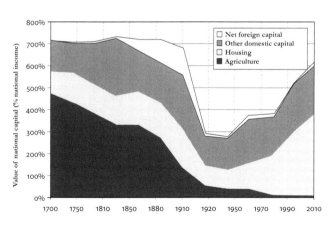

Figure 8. Capital in France, 1700–2010

The United States, on the other hand, is clearly different in a way that is not surprising on closer consideration. The development is shown in Figure 9 (Figure 4.6 in Piketty). The lack of historically accumulated capital meant that the capital/income ratio for the late eighteenth and early nineteenth centuries was low. And if we consider the asset that accounted for most of the capital stock in Europe, namely land, it was an asset in plentiful supply. These differences were noted by Alexis de Tocqueville in 1840 when, in his renowned comparison

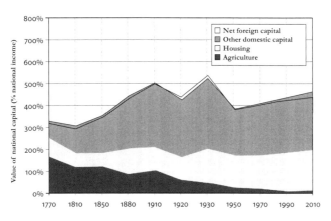

Figure 9. Capital in the United States, 1770–2010

between aristocratic and class-bound Europe and the free and egalitarian United States, he wrote: "The number of large fortunes [in the United States] is quite small, and capital is still scarce . . . In America, land costs little, and anyone can easily become a landowner."

This gradually changed and the capital stock built up in the United States during the nineteenth century. Around the turn of the twentieth century, it stood at between four and five times national income. The wars during the first half of the twentieth century had nothing like the same effect in the United States as they did in Europe (although the Great Depression as well as the participation in the Second World War had a major impact) and throughout the twentieth century the stock of capital ranged between four and five times national income.

In terms of the capital's composition, however, the trend reflects that of Europe, with agricultural land declining from just over half of all capital in the late eighteenth century to a mere fraction today. Instead, it now largely comprises buildings and other domestic capital.

Although the data for Canada do not go as far back in time and there are naturally key differences, the general picture is similar to that of the United States: a much lower level for β during the nineteenth century, a certain drop in the twentieth century (but much less than in Europe), and then a recovery in recent decades.

A general picture emerges in which Europe, where wealth was able to accumulate over a long period, had a capital/income ratio in the years before the First World War that remained steady at around six to seven times national income. Wars and various other shocks in the first half of the twentieth century more than halved the ratio up until 1950, and it has since slowly recovered to a level of four to six times national income. In stark contrast to this, β was low in the United States in the early nineteenth century. From a level of around three times national income, the ratio between capital and income then gradually rose as the stock of capital was built up during the nineteenth century, remaining at a relatively constant four to five times national income over the course of the twentieth century.

In Chapter 5, Piketty expands his analysis to include more countries. The data for these are much more recent and, for all countries studied, there seems to be a common trend since the early 1970s: a rise in the capital/income ratio. Piketty discusses many details in this development, but ultimately the core message is about the gradual rise of capital in relation to income.

• • •

So how can we explain the movements in the capital stock (K)/income flow (Y) ratio? Is it possible to understand why it ends up at a particular level and why it appears to have changed over time? It has already been suggested that the cause of the decline, particularly in Europe during the first half of the twentieth century, has to do with wars and economic crises. But why is it that the level before that remains constant at around six to seven hundred percent? Why is it that the United States did not reach this level in the nineteenth century, even if capital was accumulated? And why is it that the levels began to rise again after 1950?

Piketty explains the trend using what he calls the *second fundamental law of capitalism*, which relates the capital/income ratio to the savings rate and growth rate of the economy.

In contrast to the first "law," which is an identity, the second "law" only holds in the long run and under certain conditions. To understand this relationship, it is worth recalling the abstract model that lies behind Piketty's reasoning, where capital (in a broad sense) combines with labor to produce goods and services in the economy. What is produced in the economy forms the basis for our total incomes, which in turn can either be consumed or saved. Our savings are added to our existing capital, which thus grows or shrinks depending on whether the addition is greater or less than the capital's depreciation. (Those familiar with economic growth theory will recognize this as the basis for the so called Harrod-Domar and Solow models.)

The second fundamental law of capitalism simply states that over time the K/Y ratio will approximate the long-term saving rate, *s*, divided by the total growth in the economy over the long run, g (which is driven both by population increases and technology). That is:

$$\beta = K/Y = s/g$$

In practical terms, this means that if s = 12% and g = 2% over the long run, the ratio between capital and income will approach the level of β = 0.12/0.02 = 6. The easiest way to see why this is the case is by considering how much K and Y need to increase for the ratio to remain unchanged. Let us assume that K = 6 and Y = 1, so β = 6. If Y now increases by two percent, to 1.02, K has to increase to 6 × 1.02 = 6.12, for the ratio to remain at six. For this to happen, twelve percent of income needs to be saved. This formula also helps illustrate how it takes time to build up a stock of capital from a low level (as in the United States during the eighteenth century). If everyone saved ten percent of her income, it would take fifty years to reach a level where savings amounted to five times the level of income.

It is important to note that Piketty's law says nothing about who is saving or why. It also says nothing about why the saving rate might be five percent in one country and fifteen percent in another. Nor does it explain why one country has a growth rate of one percent and another has three percent growth, or what drives this growth. All the formula says is that *if* saving is s and overall growth is *g* then over time β will approximate *s/g*.

Nevertheless, Piketty believes the formula is useful in understanding many of the features observed in the data. The reason that the United States in the nineteenth century is so markedly different to Europe is a combination of a very low initial capital stock, the low value of land and, above all, a much higher growth rate in the United States compared with Europe. This difference is almost entirely due to differences in demographic growth. The population in France in the early nineteenth century was around thirty million and has more or less doubled since then. In Britain the figure was just over twenty million and has more or less trebled. In the United States, the population in the early nineteenth century stood at around ten million but has since grown by a factor of around thirty. This difference amounts to around one percentage point's difference in economic growth over two hundred years.

With saving at around ten to twelve percent, economic growth of around 1.5 to two percent over the long run, as in Europe, equates to a long-term β of six to eight times national income. If the economic growth rate averages 2.5–3 percent per year, instead, β approaches three to four times national income. Right in line with the differences we observe in the data.

As mentioned previously, the steep decline in the first half of the twentieth century can largely be explained by the wars, but also by other factors such as financial regulation and a political climate that did not favor capital accumulation. The fact that the recovery takes time is also not surprising and the faster pace of the recovery since 1980 compared with the period 1950–1980 chimes well with the downturn in the growth rate over the past thirty years compared with the rapid growth of the post-war period.

All these approximate relationships naturally conceal many contributory details (as discussed by Piketty). For instance, in the analysis of the trend since 1970, the period for which we are able to observe many countries, Piketty notes major differences in private savings across countries, and also changes in the composition between public and private capital. At times, various financial bubbles have also influenced the relationship between capital and income. But overall, Piketty believes the major trends over the long run can be satisfactorily explained by the relationship between savings and growth.

• • •

The fluctuations in the capital/income ratio do not in themselves say anything about the income share going to aggregate capital and labor respectively, or about the distribution of incomes across individuals. (The individual income distribution is the focus of Part Three of the book.) But if we focus on the division of income between capital and labor, we can combine our understanding of what determines β over the long run—that is, the ratio s/g—with the *first fundamental law of capitalism* to see what determines the capital-labor split. The first law states that the capital share of national income, α, is the product of the rate of return on capital, r, and the capital income ratio, β, i.e., $\alpha = r \times \beta$. If we know what determines β, we need to understand what determines r to understand how incomes are divided between capital and labor. What determines the rate of return on capital, r, is the main issue in Chapter 6.

Piketty begins by looking at historical data in Britain and France, again because these are the countries for which we have the best historical data. The development of the capital-labor split in these countries is shown in Figures 10 and 11 (corresponding to

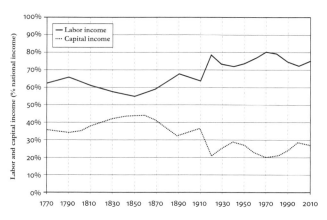

Figure 10. The capital-labor split in Britain, 1770–2010

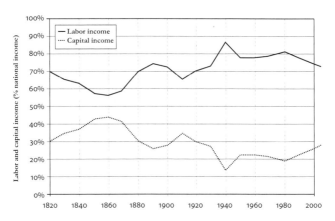

Figure 11. The capital-labor split in France, 1820–2010

Figures 6.1. and 6.2. in Piketty's book). He first notes that our direct observations of the capital share, α, displays the same U-shaped pattern over time as the capital/income share, β, but with less dramatic fluctuations. This suggests that the rate of return on capital, *r*, has been lower at times when β is high and vice versa, which seems plausible. When capital is plentiful, the rate of return on capital is lower.

Piketty then attempts to estimate the size of *r* directly. His results for Britain and France are shown in

Figures 12 and 13 (Figures 6.3. and 6.4. in *Capital*). The calculation is done by working out an average based on capital income from various sources. Clearly, there is a lot of variation in returns across different types of capital but in the end Piketty concludes that the average rate has fluctuated around four to five percent since the end of the eighteenth century, without any clear long-run trend in any direction.

Based on these historical observations, Piketty goes on to explain how the rate of return on capital is

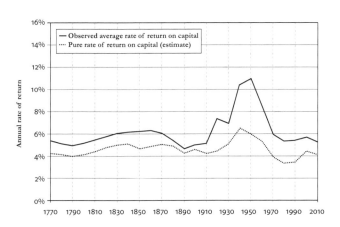

Figure 12. The pure rate of return on capital in Britain, 1770–2010

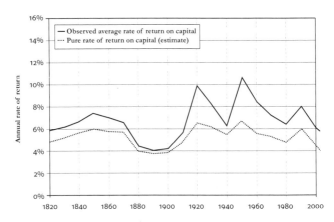

Figure 13. The pure rate of return on capital in France, 1820–2010

determined in economic theory. He begins by pointing out that the rate of return obviously should depend on the amount of capital. When there is plenty of capital, and the capital/income ratio is high, the return to capital is lower than when the opposite is true. The question is, however, which effect dominates in the determination of the capital share of income, α.

If the stock of capital increases in relation to the income flow, there is more capital around to generate capital income, but if, at the same time, the return on capital falls, the overall effect depends on which of the changes has the largest impact on the capital share.

The answer relates to what economists call the *elasticity of substitution* between capital and labor. In simple terms, this means the degree to which a reduction (or increase) in capital can be substituted by more (or less) labor. Taken to one extreme, an increase in capital (or labor) has no effect if labor (or capital) is not increased at the same time. To give an example, if one hundred people have one hundred shovels, one additional shovel does nothing unless there is also an additional person to use it. In such a case, the elasticity of substitution is said to be zero. Capital cannot replace labor. At the other extreme, labor and capital are entirely independent of each other. Production can be increased by adding capital without increasing labor, and there is no reduction in productivity no matter how much capital one has. For an example of such a situation, imagine an entirely robotized economy in which one can increase production at will simply by adding more robots. In this situation, the elasticity of substitution is infinite.

Neither of these extremes is of relevance in practice, or in answering the question of whether the return on capital dominates changes in the capital/income ratio, β. The important question is whether the elasticity of substitution between labor and capital is greater or less than one. If it is between zero and one, then an increase in β leads to a decrease in r large enough that the capital share $\alpha = r \times \beta$ decreases (given that r is determined by the marginal productivity of the capital). If, on the other hand, the elasticity is greater than one, the effect of an increase in β will lead to a decrease in r, but the capital share $\alpha = r \times \beta$ will still increase. If the elasticity is exactly equal to one, then we have a special case that often appears in economic models, where the two effects cancel each other out. A decrease in r exactly offsets the increase in β, such that α remains unchanged (economists call this the Cobb-Douglas production function).

Piketty explains why the notion of α being relatively constant has become so common in the world of economics, particularly in textbooks. This is due in part to its accessible simplification of reality, but also to the fact that many earlier studies over shorter historical periods have indicated a relatively stable relationship. Since the 1990s, however, numerous studies have shown that the distribution between capital and labor appears to have risen since the 1970s, and in the 2000s organizations such as the IMF and the OECD published several reports highlighting the phenomenon.

The novelty of this part of Piketty's study is that, as he explained, it is the first attempt to study the long-run evolution of the capital-labor split within national income. By placing the increases of the recent decades in a historical perspective that stretches back over the past two centuries, we can gain a whole new basis on which to study the split between capital income and income from labor. From this perspective, rather than remaining stable, the relationship has fluctuated over time, from historically high levels in the early nineteenth century, when the capital share α was thirty-five to forty percent, to historically low levels of twenty to twenty-five percent around 1970 and today's figure of twenty-five to thirty percent.

• • •

According to Piketty, the key conclusion from all this is there is no natural force that inevitably reduces the importance of capital over time. The idea that human capital might replace nonhuman capital as the economy develops is not borne out by the data. Economic growth is driven in the long run by productivity and knowledge, which has made it possible to avoid the apocalypse predicted by Marx of constant capital accumulation as the only driver of growth. Technological progress has no doubt increased the demand for knowledge and skills, but it has also increased demand for all the various forms of nonhuman capital. Overall, economic development has not reduced the importance of capital and there is no reason to believe it will automatically lead to a reduced role for capital in relation to labor in the future.

PART THREE:
THE STRUCTURE OF
INEQUALITY

So far, the discussion has been about large-scale social abstractions, such as total capital and its relation to all income, the relationship between capital income and income from labor, total savings, the return on capital, and the average growth rate in the economy. It is tempting to move directly from these relationships to drawing conclusions at an individual level. Based on the archetypal capital owner earning money on his capital, and the worker who only has his wages, the aggregate differences in total capital income and income from labor translate directly to individual outcomes. It was in these terms that economists such as Marx considered the issue: the distribution of national income directly reflected the tension between workers and capitalists. If there was any change in the distribution, it directly benefited the one group at the expense of the other. Taking such a view, one can also see how a constant distribution between labor and capital, i.e., a constant α, removes this tension at a stroke. The shares are kept fixed due to the production function and the distribution is not dependent on any "class struggle," but is provided by a technological constant. The question of distribution between total capital and total income then becomes irrelevant for the individual income distribution.

Basing an argument on a perspective in which capital is set against labor is, however, potentially problematic, since it ignores the fact that most of us actually have both income from labor and capital income to a varying extent. There are, of course, people who earn a great deal from their private capital, and there are people who have no private capital income at all (and we will return to the consequences of this over time). The reasons for such inequalities may in turn be due to a whole host of factors. The size of a personal fortune varies with age, but it also differs a great deal between people at the same stage in life. Its origin may be work and savings or inheritance. The distribution also depends on how capital ownership is organized in society. For example, in a country such as Sweden, with considerable public pension assets, people who have no private assets may benefit from capital growth, despite this not being expressed as private capital income.

Even more importantly, in practice there is of course not just one type of worker, just as there is not one kind of capital owner. The differences within and between the distributions can be quite substantial. A person with a small fortune and no job may have a much lower income than a person in a well-paid job or a successful entrepreneur, even though the first is a "capitalist" and the second a "worker."

In short, the distribution of income between capital and labor may not say anything about economic inequality between individuals. Theoretically, it is just as possible for the individual distribution to become more equal if the wage share of income increases as it is for the inequality to increase in the same circumstances. It all depends on the *individual distribution of income from labor and capital*, and the next step is therefore to study how income and wealth are distributed between individuals. This is the theme for part three of *Capital in the Twenty-First Century*.

• • •

Piketty begins by suggesting that economic inequality between individuals may stem from three different sources: inequality in income from labor, inequality in the ownership of capital and the income to which it gives rise, and the interaction between these two terms. Once again, the argument is illustrated with reference to Balzac's novel *Père Goriot*, which captures the possible routes to personal riches. Despite his wealth, in his twilight years Père Goriot lives in a simple boarding-house, since he has chosen to spend his wealth on creating the best possible opportunities for his daughters to rise in the Parisian high society. At the boarding-house Goriot meets the penniless young Eugéne de Rastignac, who has come to Paris from the provinces to study law. Full of ambition, he plans to climb the social ladder through study and hard work, but he soon discovers no matter how successful he is in his studies, his prospects of achieving a real fortune are limited. This reality is spelled out to him with great precision by Vautrin, a dubious character who also lives at the boarding-house. He suggests that instead of focusing on his education, Rastignac should marry the wealthy Mademoiselle Victorine. According to Vautrin, this would immediately bring him a fortune of one million francs, and thus an annual income of 50,000 francs (a five percent return on the capital). This is much more than he would be able to earn after years of study and on a par with the best he could earn at the end of a long career—assuming he became an extremely successful lawyer. This is what Piketty described as "Rastignac's dilemma": to study and work hard and in the best case achieve success later in life or, in the absence of an inheritance, marry into money.

According to Piketty, this episode illustrates two things: firstly, how clear it must have been to Balzac's contemporaries how taken for granted it was that wealth generated income and what figures were involved, and secondly how difficult—not to say impossible—it was in a lifetime to achieve a wage that could match the return on a large fortune. These circumstances—in which large fortunes generated larger incomes than even the best paid workers could hope to achieve—applied, according to Piketty, across practically the whole of Europe up until the early twentieth century.

Most of us feel, intuitively, that Rastignac's dilemma belongs to the past. There can be situations where inheritance or marriage is more profitable, but in today's society education, work, and climbing the career ladder are better paths to success. The question is how can we know that income from labor really is more important than income from inherited wealth? And even more importantly: why and when did such a change occur?

• • •

To answer these questions, we need to study various aspects of the individual distribution for income from labor and from capital, and the distribution of wealth. To discuss these issues, we also require measures that capture different degrees of inequality.

There are many approaches that can be taken, all of which have their pros and cons. By far the most common measure for capturing differences in distribution is the Gini coefficient. This is a convenient measure in that it offers a single number to represent the distribution in society. It is designed such that the Gini coefficient is one if one person has all the income or holds the entire wealth of society, and it is zero if everyone in society has exactly the same share of income or wealth. The reality will, of course, always fall somewhere between these extremes. To gain a sense of scale, the Gini coefficient for incomes in Sweden today is around 0.3 while in the United States it is just over 0.4. Wealth is much less equally distributed, and this appears to be the case in all the countries and all the periods for which we have data. The Gini coefficient for wealth ranges between 0.6 and 0.8.

But what does a change in the Gini coefficient from 0.3 to 0.4 actually mean? Apart from knowing what the figure is for countries whose conditions we are familiar with, it is hard to get an intuitive sense of what is actually being represented. There is also another key problem: the Gini coefficient says nothing about *where in the distribution the changes occur.* There is a major difference between a trend that is driven by the richest half of the population receiving more or less compared with the poorest, and a change in which a small group gains more or less relative to everyone else. These respective changes will, in all likelihood, be due to completely different mechanisms, but the difference may not be apparent in the Gini coefficient.

According to Piketty, it is therefore better to focus on measures that are easier to understand intuitively, separating out the trend for different parts of the distribution. Naturally, this entails looking at more than one figure, but the effort is rewarded with a clearer picture of the changes that take place. Piketty's preferred measure is *the share of the total earned by a particular group in the distribution.* For incomes, for example, he calculates the share of all income earned by the tenth of the population with the highest incomes (the top ten percent), or the share of all incomes earned by those at the very top of the distribution (the top one percent). Similarly, the wealth distribution is presented in terms of the share of wealth owned by the top ten percent, or the top one percent. The reason why the historical series are limited to these top groups is a lack of individual data for most of the population as we move back in time. Since only high-income earners paid taxes initially, the early information is restricted to them. We do, however, have data on aggregate income for the whole population. This makes it possible to calculate the top groups' share of the total.

As mentioned, income derives either from labor or from capital, and separating out these sources proves vital in understanding the economic inequalities in society. In some cases the focus is on the top shares of all labor income, in others it is the top shares of all capital income, but in most cases, the focus is on top shares of income form all sources.

Finally, when looking at these series, it is important to remember that the population share refers to the share of the whole adult population and the income share to income before tax and transfers. Of course, a great deal has happened in terms of taxation and redistribution over the time. But it is also worth noting it is by no means clear in what direction such changes would take the overall trend. For countries and periods when we can observe both top shares, as measured by Piketty, and other indicators of inequality, such as the Gini coefficient for disposable income (that is, after taxes and transfers) these move in similar ways over time. This suggests that even if we only can observe top shares over the long run, this may not be a bad proxy for general trends in inequality.

How does the distribution of income and wealth change over time? What role does income from labor play compared with capital income? What character-izes the rise in income inequality that appears to have taken place in recent decades, and how does this relate to historical levels?

Piketty begins by studying the income distribu-tion over the twentieth century, using data from France and the United States. This time, the main reason for choosing these countries is not that they have better data than other countries (as was the case for France and Britain in the study of the capital/income ratio). Instead, these countries can, respectively, be said to represent what in this field of research has been referred to as the Continental European and Anglo-Saxon experience. Hence, the title of Chapter 8 in Piketty's book, *Two Worlds*, which accounts for this development. Again, there are obviously many details that are not captured by this division but, as we will see, the split does reveal some important patterns.

• • •

Let us begin with the trend in France. Figure 14 (Piketty 8.1) shows the top ten percent's share of total income over the twentieth century, together with the top ten percent's share of all wage income. The figure shows that while the top group's share of total income falls sharply in the first half of the century, especially around World War II, the wage share of the top ten group in the wage distribution remains relatively stable throughout. This shows that the main reason behind the fall of the top ten group's income share comes from shrinking capital incomes for the top group in connection to the war.

Figure 15 (8.2 in *Capital*) shows a corresponding trend for the top one percent in the income and wage distribution in France over the twentieth century. The trend

Figure 14. Income inequality in France, 1910–2010

is even clearer here, in that the top one percent's share of income falls steadily for the whole period up until the end of the Second World War. The sharpest drop comes with the advent of war, but the downturn in the late 1920s and early 1930s is also clear. At the same time, the top one percent's share of the wage distribution remained fairly constant throughout the twentieth century.

Together these figures illustrate two key points. First, much of what happens to the top income shares in France over the twentieth century is driven by a

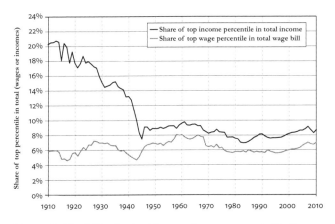

Figure 15. The fall in the significance of return on capital in France, 1910–2010

sharp and at times concentrated decline in capital income, while the wage distribution trend for top groups shows little change. Second, much of what happens is heavily concentrated in the top one percent. Of the total drop in the top ten percent's share of income between 1910 and 1945, around sixteen percentage points, the top one percent accounts for around twelve percentage points.

Let us now compare this trend with that in the United States. Figure 16 (Piketty 8.5) shows the top ten percent's share of income over the twentieth century. In the American data, it is possible to separate out realized capital gains, which is why two different lines of the development can be drawn. This has no effect, however, on the overall trend. In the United States, just as in France, we see an extreme fall in the top ten percent's share of income during the Second World War, but we also see a precipitous rise starting around 1980. Over the past thirty-five years, the income share of the top ten percent has risen to levels not seen in the United

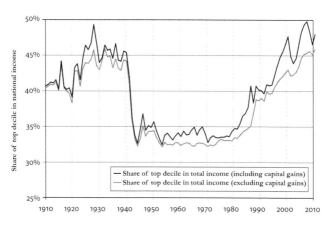

Figure 16. Income inequality in the United States, 1910–2010

States since the 1920s. This rise is very different from what we see in France over the recent decades.

Over the whole period, the countries show a similar development, in terms of both level and trend, up until 1980, after which top income shares shoot up in the United States, while remaining relatively stable in France.

If we look at how much of the change is attributable to the different parts of the top group (Figure 17, corresponding to 8.6 in Piketty), we can see that in the

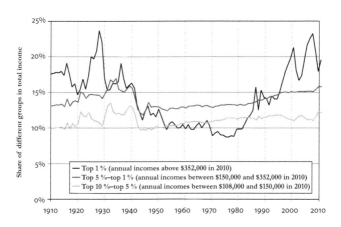

Figure 17. Income distribution in the top ten percent in the United States, 1910–2010

United States too the development is mostly a top one percent phenomenon, although the rest of the top ten percent (P90–95 and P95–99) also gradually increased their share. Looking at changes in income composition, it is clear that, as in France, the top share in the United States falls most due to diminishing capital income during the Second World War. The wage share for the top ten percent also declines over the war years, but by nowhere near as much. The upturn after 1980 in the United States, however, appears to have little to do with capital. Figure 18 (Piketty 8.7) shows how much of the increased top ten income share since the 1970s is related to increasing top wages. As the top decile's income share in total income goes from just below thirty-five percent in the mid 1970s to just above forty-five percent in 2010, the top wage decile increases its share in the total wage bill from just above twenty-five percent to around thirty-five percent over the same period. This indicates that most of the change in the United States over the past decades has come from larger wage inequality.

Expanding the perspective to other countries, the trends in France and the United States can be said to

Figure 18. High incomes and high wages in the United States, 1910–2010

represent the evolution of top income shares in two groups of countries, namely Continental European and Anglo-Saxon countries respectively. Figure 19 (9.2 in *Capital*) shows the trend for the top one percent in four Anglo-Saxon countries: Australia, Canada, Britain, and the United States. All these show a similar pattern of falling top income shares, mostly in conjunction with the Second World War, up until around 1980, when the top one percent's share of income sees an upturn and increases significantly toward the present day.

Figure 20 (Piketty 9.3) shows the corresponding trend in France, Germany, Sweden, and Japan. All these countries also show a gradual downturn in the top one percent's share of income up until around 1980. The greatest decline coincides with the Second World War in France and Germany, while the change is less dramatic in Sweden. After 1980, there is a certain rise—in percentage terms quite a strong rise in Sweden—but the

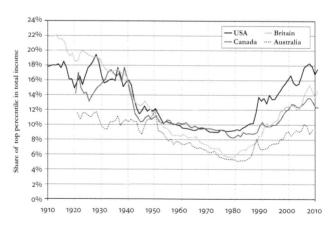

Figure 19. Income inequality in Anglo-Saxon countries, 1910–2010

difference compared with the Anglo-Saxon countries is still striking.

How do we interpret this trend? According to Piketty, the first part, the fall in top income shares over the first eighty years of the twentieth century, particularly its first half, is clear. The decline in top incomes is linked to diminishing income in the top one percent, and is so strongly dominated by steep falls in capital income that the only reasonable explanation is the destruction of capital, directly in conjunction with war but also as

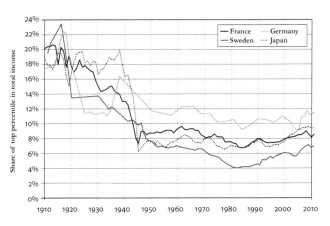

Figure 20. Income inequality in Continental Europe and Japan, 1910–2010

a consequence of political decisions concerning taxation and the nationalization of assets. High marginal income tax rates in the decades following the Second World War then held back high wages and the recovery of capital.

When it comes to the rising income inequality in recent decades, primarily in the Anglo-Saxon countries, Piketty suggests some of that development can be related to technological progress increasing demand for highly skilled labor. Unless the education system keeps pace and increases supply as demand rises, such a trend will lead to greater wage inequality between those with and without a good education. However, there are aspects of the trend that cannot be explained by this theory, particularly the fact that so much of the rising income inequality is concentrated at the top of the distribution. When supply and demand for skilled labor is the determining factor, inequalities grow between larger groups, the educated and the less educated. But this does not explain why a small group within the educated group has come to earn so much more than others. The so-called superstar-theories often put forward to explain the increased concentration within the top of the distribution are not Piketty's preferred explanations. Instead he emphasizes changing social norms regarding what constitutes reasonable remuneration (especially in the United States) which has enabled top wages to increase sharply.

What about the distribution of wealth? How has this developed over time? An understanding of this is important in itself, but also because so much of the levelling of income equality during the twentieth century appears to have been driven by capital income. Although the data for wealth are much more problematic than those for income, and long-run historical information is only available for a handful of countries, certain clear changes can be discerned over time.

In many ways, the picture that emerges reflects the trend of the capital/income ratio as presented in the second part of the book. The concentration of wealth appears to have been high and relatively stable in nineteenth-century France and Britain. In all these countries, the top ten percent owned 80–90 percent of the private assets (a much greater proportion than the corresponding top group in the income distribution).

However, this share declined sharply over the twentieth century up to around 1970, after which a certain recovery may be discernible.

As with the evolution of the capital/income ratio, the trend and, in particular, the levels differ between the United States and Europe. In the United States, the nineteenth century appears to have been a time of gradually increasing wealth concentration, which Piketty suggests is a natural reflection of the lack of historically

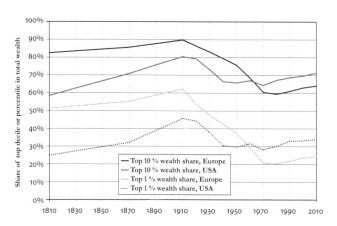

Figure 21. Wealth inequality in Europe versus United States, 1810–2010

accumulated wealth. The concentration of wealth does fall in the United States over the twentieth century, but not as much as it does in Europe. In recent decades, there are signs that the concentration has once again increased somewhat. Figure 21 (Piketty 10.6) shows the top ten percent and top one percent wealth shares in Europe (calculated as an average of these shares in France, Britain and Sweden) compared to the corresponding developments in the United States over the period 1810–2010.

• • •

Let us now try to explain what we observe: a hyper-concentration of wealth in nineteenth century Europe; a sharp decline in times of war and other shocks over the period 1914–1945; and the fact that this concentration of wealth has not—as yet—returned to the very high levels of the past.

There are, of course, a host of different factors behind this development, but one relationship stands out as most important: the one between the average rate of return on capital, *r*, and the average rate of growth in the economy, *g* (from both demographic growth and productivity growth). The most important factor behind the high wealth concentration in Europe before 1900, and to a large extent in all societies with the exception of the pioneer societies of the New World, which are not representative of the rest of the world or the long run, is that *the rate of return on capital over the long run has been much higher than the rate of growth.* This difference constitutes a fundamental force that, under certain assumptions, increases inequality over time.

The explanation is as follows: consider an economy with a growth rate of one percent ($g = 1\%$), and a rate of return on capital of five percent ($r = 5\%$). Saving one fifth of the income from capital (while consuming the other four fifths) is enough to ensure that the capital inherited from the previous generation grows at the same rate as the economy. If one saves more, then one's fortune will increase more rapidly than the overall economy, even without adding income from labor. As a consequence the conditions are ideal for what Piketty calls an "inheritance society" character-ized by both a very high concentration of wealth and a significant persistence of large fortunes from generation to generation.

As already discussed (specifically in Chapters 2 and 6 of *Capital in the Twenty-First Century*), the time before the Industrial Revolution featured a very low rate of economic growth, while the annual rate of return on capital is thought to have been 4–5 percent. The economy then grew significantly in the nineteenth century, but the difference compared with the average return on capital remained considerable. During the conditions that prevailed at the time, when capital income accounted for around 40 percent of all income, just saving a quarter of this would ensure that wealth grew more quickly than income, resulting in a rising concentration of wealth.

During the first half of the twentieth century, this picture changed dramatically. War, taxation, and a series of economic shocks not only cut the average return on capital, but also destroyed much of the capital stock (although the return before taxes and capital losses remained around five percent). During the post-war years, taxes dampened the return on capital for a while, but the main feature of this period was strong growth. Annual growth rates of three to four percent have led to "new money" dominating "inherited wealth." According to Piketty, however, all this is set to change in the future. For one thing, the growth rate is likely to fall, not least due to lower demographic growth, and for another, the rate of return on capital is likely to be a good bit higher. Piketty believes some of this is due to competition for capital between countries forcing down taxes on it. In his future projections, he therefore assumes a tax rate on capital of ten percent for the period 2012–2050 and zero percent for 2050–2100 (the average capital tax for 1913–2012 is set at 30 percent). Once again, the point is made that things are much more complicated in practice, with huge variations between countries, over time, and between different types of capital. Nevertheless, Piketty asserted that the assumptions and their consequences capture the main forces of the underlying long-run trend.

Figure 22 (Piketty 10.10) summarizes the evolution that Piketty sees as most crucial in understanding the long-run trend in inequality. Throughout history,

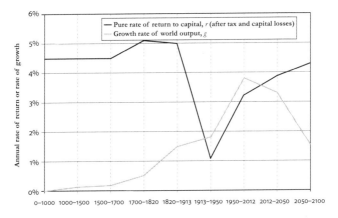

Figure 22. After tax rate of return versus growth rate at the world level, from Antiquity until 2100

$r > g$ until the first half of the twentieth century, when a combination of wars and economic shocks drives down the pure rate of return to capital so that the relation is reversed and $g > r$. This is followed by a period of historically high economic growth which keeps $g > r$ up until present day.

This may, however, change in the near future, both through g falling and r rising relative to twentieth century levels. As previously discussed in Section 2, g is likely to fall at least in its demographic component, and the development of r depends on how it responds when capital grows. Piketty repeatedly stresses that nothing is certain in future developments. In the end, however, his view of the relationship between r and g seen through the lens of historical fact, rather than logical necessity, makes his conclusion clear: a return to $r > g$ in the future seems likely.

What does this mean for the evolution of individual wealth distribution? And how does it relate to the possible return of inherited wealth? There are naturally a large number of factors at play here. Individual fortunes are created and destroyed, through competence and incompetence, good luck and bad. Rules on inheritance also affect how and whether a fortune is split up over time. With an equal split between heirs, initially large fortunes can be spread thinly among many individuals over the course of a few generations. This does not happen if, for example, the eldest son inherits everything, but low demographic growth also has a limiting effect. In some cases, individual fortunes are affected by factors specific to them, while at other times everyone in society may be affected, as in the case of war. It can, however, be shown that if individual fortunes are randomly affected by both specific and general shocks of various kinds, the distribution of wealth is driven towards increased concentration as the difference between r and g grows. Of course, this says nothing about the development of individual fortunes, but it illustrates that, under quite general assumptions, wealth tends to become more concentrated, the greater the difference between the rate of return on capital and the rate of growth in the economy.

In Chapter 11 of the book, Piketty asks how great an inheritance flow we can actually observe and how this has changed over time. It is important to study this, since it is entirely possible the capital/income ratio may be of any size without this affecting how much is inherited in each generation. If everyone in society works and saves money when they are young, and then consumes everything in older age, there will be no fortunes to inherit. Everyone will begin life on the same terms (as far as inherited money is concerned) and then work to build up capital over a lifetime that they then consume later in life; this idea is often referred to as the "life-cycle hypothesis." On the other hand, if all individuals accumulate money that is not consumed over their lifetime, whether from inheritance or their own labor, they will inevitably die with a fortune that will then be inherited by someone.

Two questions we might want to ask now are: first, how large are inheritance flows in relation to other incomes, and second, how has this changed over time? Piketty studied these questions in the case of France, the only country so far for which such information is available, over the period 1820–2010. Given the underlying data there are basically two ways to estimate inheritance flows. The first is to directly observe all bequests, sum these up, add all gifts, and then relate the values to income for each year. The flow based on such observations is called the "fiscal flow" (since it typically derives from data generated in the taxation of inheritances and gifts). The other way is to estimate the size of all private wealth (which in contrast to public assets can be inherited) in relation to income, and then try to estimate how much wealth a person on average has at the time of death compared with the average for the living population, and finally to calculate how common it is for a person to die. Based on these three components, it is possible to work out the inheritance flow using the formula,

$$b = \beta \times \mu \times m$$

where b is the annual economic flow of inheritances and gifts expressed as a proportion of national income, β is the ratio of total private wealth to national income, μ is the ratio of average wealth at the time of death to the average wealth of living individuals, and m is the mortality rate. This flow is called the "economic flow." The intuition is simple: if the amount of private wealth is three times national income, those who die are twice as rich as the living population on average, and the mortality rate is two percent, the inheritance flow will be $3 \times 2 \times 0.02 = 0.12$, or twelve percent. If the stock of private wealth grows to six times national income, the flow will instead be $6 \times 2 \times 0.02 = 0.24$. The inheritance flow has thus taken on greater significance due to the stock of private capital increasing in relation to income. If older people instead consume much of their fortune in their later years so that the average wealth of those who die is the same as the wealth in the living population, the flow instead becomes $6 \times 1 \times 0.02 = 0.12$. The significance of inheritance thus falls despite an increase in the stock of private capital. In the extreme case where older people consume everything before they die, μ approaches zero and the significance of inheritance heads towards zero, irrespective of what β (or m) may be.

This formula is not dependent on any assumptions. In fact it is a pure accounting identity, just like the *first*

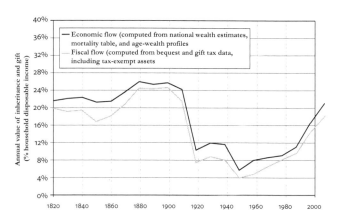

Figure 23. The annual inheritance flow expressed as a fraction of disposable household income in France, 1820–2010

fundamental law of capitalism. This does not mean that the results are in any way either trivial or certain. The relations needed to apply the formula are difficult to estimate over time. However, the ability to estimate inheritance flow in two ways lends greater robustness to the results.

Figure 23 (Piketty 11.8) illustrates Piketty's computations of annual inheritance flow as a fraction of national income in France, based on both the "fiscal flow" and the "economic flow" for the period 1820–2010.

Both methods provide a similar picture. Inheritance flows were significant, at around twenty to twenty-five percent of national income, throughout the nineteenth century and then fell sharply in the early twentieth century, but they have rebounded in recent decades and are approaching nineteenth century levels.

• • •

In the final chapter of Part Three (Chapter 12 in *Capital*), Piketty uses the scarce data that is available to discuss what we can learn from studying the truly large fortunes. His main conclusion from this analysis is that the truly large fortunes, such as those listed in magazines such as *Forbes* and in reports such as the so-called *Global Wealth Reports*, generally appear to be growing more quickly than the average rate of return on capital. This is not particularly surprising, but it is nevertheless a potentially important factor that amplifies the $r > g$ dynamic, increasing the return on capital at the top of the distribution.

Piketty also points out that the fact that many fortunes at the top of these lists are created by the individuals themselves does not change his basic argument. Naturally, suggested Piketty, entrepreneurship and innovation are important for society, but no matter how well deserved wealth may be initially, over time it can grow in a way that is indefensible in terms of social justice.

PART FOUR: REGULATING CAPITAL IN THE TWENTY-FIRST CENTURY

The first three parts of *Capital in the Twenty-First Century* examine the distribution of income and wealth in society, with a focus on their evolution since the nineteenth century. In the fourth and final part of the book, Piketty attempts to draw lessons for the future based on the historical trends he observes. Given that the single greatest mechanism for levelling out income and wealth over the twentieth century was war and destruction of capital, rather than a natural tendency for inequality to go down as the economy develops, and given that inequality now appears to be rising, he asks what we can do about it. Can we imagine political institutions that might regulate today's capitalism justly as well as efficiently? Or do we have to wait for the next crisis or, in the worst case, the next war?

As already suggested earlier in the book, the ideal policy according to Piketty would be to introduce a progressive global tax on capital. Such a tax would also have the benefit of generating more information and transparency about the size and distribution of wealth. In addition, Piketty believes it would promote the general interest over private interests while preserving economic openness and the forces of competition. The alternative, as he sees it, is a trend toward increased protectionism and a less dynamic economy. Piketty states that a global tax on capital is utopian, but cooperation between a limited number of countries could be an effective alternative.

In discussing the options, it is important to understand the role of the state in supporting fundamental social rights and to understand how taxation in society has evolved. This is the focus of Chapters 13 and 14. The key points of Chapter 13 are that the size of the state in terms of the burden of taxation grew during the twentieth century and that the role of the state has remained more or less the same over the past few decades. The discussion of future reforms is thus not about changing the size of the state, in the first instance. As ever, there are considerable variations from country to country but, in broad terms, countries such as Sweden and the United States have more commonalities than differences. The state's primary undertakings in areas such as health care and pensions and, above all, the role of education in ensuring that everyone has equal opportunities, are based on principles of social justice, and there are no obvious arguments either for reducing or increasing these undertakings. There are, though, many good reasons for reforms in various directions, with different countries facing differing challenges. With respect to the long-run challenges in focus here, it is not the basic role of the state nor the size of government that needs to change.

Chapter 14 discusses the structure of taxes and the specific idea of a progressive tax on both income and inheritances. Once again, Piketty looks to history and finds that the wars in the first half of the twentieth century played a central role in the creation and evolution of taxes. It is true that many countries intro-duced progressive income tax in the late nineteenth and early twentieth centuries, but the levels were very low, and only rose dramatically with the advent of the First World War. He also notes that Britain and par-ticularly the United States were much more progressive than many European countries in introducing high tax rates on high incomes and large inheritances. Many people in the United States were concerned about the huge wealth inequalities of the early twentieth century, and felt that the trend threatened the very foundations of American society. A heavy progressive inheritance tax was an obvious solution to stop a trend in which wealth inequality had become "undemocratic," with the United States steadily becoming more like inheri-tance-dominated Europe, according to leading econo-mist Irving Fisher, for example.

For decades, both during and after the war, the United States and Britain had the most progressive tax systems, with top rates of around eighty to ninety per-cent on incomes, compared with levels of around fifty to sixty percent in France and Germany. Around 1980, however, there was a radical change. The top rates in Britain and the United States fell to thirty to forty percent, while the rates in France and Germany remained more or less the same. These changes in the top marginal tax rate show a close correlation with the income share of the top one percent. The countries with the greatest reductions in the top marginal tax rate have also seen the greatest increase in top salaries. Piketty sees no signs of this leading to increased productivity. He does, however, find it plausible that a top manager who only receives a small share of any wage increase above a certain level has much less incentive to hike up his or her salary than someone who retains the majority of any such increase. Piketty thus sees raising the top marginal tax rate as the most obvious solution to reign in the extreme executive salaries found primarily in the United States. He is, however, not particularly optimistic about the chances of such a change occurring. The egalitarian and pioneering ideal of American society has been lost and the New World may be on the verge of becoming the Old Europe of the twenty-first century, as he puts it.

In Chapter 15 of *Capital*, Piketty discusses the proposal that he sees, at least in terms of principle, as the best way to check the spiral of increasing inequality we otherwise risk getting caught up in—a progressive global tax on capital. Despite it being utopian, he thinks it useful as a standard against which other, more realistic, alternatives can be measured. So, if we ignore the practicalities for a moment, what would the tax look like in principle? To start with, the tax would be applied to net wealth, which is the value of all assets (financial and nonfinancial) minus debt. The rate might be in the order of zero percent for net assets of less than one million euros, one percent for assets of one to five million and two percent above five million. It is important to note that such a tax would differ from the related taxes that are already applied in many countries. In contrast to property taxes, for example, the tax on capital takes account not only of real property but all assets, and it is also not based on the value of the asset, but on net assets. A person in debt should not pay the same amount as a person with no debt. When it comes to revenue from the tax (disregarding practical issues and potential evasion), it should never generate more than modest revenues, a few points of national income perhaps. The primary point of the tax is not to provide a source of revenue, but to rein in the spiral of inequality that otherwise risks occurring, and at the same time create a clear picture of wealth ownership in society. The latter point is important, since it is hard to discuss a number of leading issues when knowledge about the ownership of wealth is so difficult to obtain. It is also important to note that a tax on capital in many ways complements income taxes and inheritance taxes in what might be called the ideal tax system. To illustrate just one of many points: imagine that a wealthy person has a fortune of ten billion and that over the course of a year this increases in value by five percent (500 million). In economic terms this means that the person has received an income of 500 million, since economic income is defined as *the amount a person can afford to spend during a given period, and be as well-off at the end of it as at its beginning.* In practice and for tax purposes it is, however, more likely that the person in question will declare an income that is a fraction of this, say five million, and pay tax on that. This is not tax evasion, simply a reflection of the fact that without a complementary tax on capital, it is probable that extremely wealthy individuals will, in practice, only pay tax on a very small part of the economic income they receive.

Could such a tax be introduced, if not globally, then perhaps at European level? Thomas Piketty sees no reason why not. A system of the type outlined above, with a tax rate of 0.1 percent on net wealth below 200,000 euros, for instance, and 0.5 percent on wealth of between 200,000 and 1 million, would be able to replace property tax (where it exists), which is practically a wealth tax on the propertied middle class. A system that also then applied a tax rate of one percent on wealth of between one and five million euros, and two percent on anything above that, would generate revenues in the order of two percent of Europe's GDP. Such a system would, of course, require changes to Europe's political institutions, but it would be the best way to tackle the increasing concentration of wealth and its consequences.

CONCLUSION

As with the introduction to the book, it can seem superfluous to include its conclusions in a summary. It is, however, interesting to see what Piketty picked out as the main lessons from his research.

He begins by once again emphasizing that *Capital in the Twenty-First Century* draws on more extensive material about the actual historical trends than has been available to any previous author, while also conceding that this material is, of its very nature, imperfect and incomplete. He also stresses that his conclusions are tenuous and deserve to be questioned, and also it is not the purpose of social science research to produce mathematical certainties that can substitute for open, democratic debate.

The overall conclusion of the book, according to Piketty, is that a market economy based on private property contains powerful forces that push in the direction of increased inequality as well as forces that push in the other direction.

The force with the clearest power to level out inequality, both between countries and individuals, is the increased diffusion of knowledge and skills. According to Piketty, the most powerful force in the other direction, and the one that has been the focus of the book, is the fact that the private rate of return on capital, r, can be significantly higher for long periods of time than the rate of economic growth, g. This central inequality, $r > g$, implies that wealth accumulated in the past grows more rapidly than output and wages. And where capital is concentrated, it grows more quickly than income from labor, thus increasing inequalities over time.

One solution could be to tax capital income heavily enough to reduce the private return on capital to less than the growth rate. Such a solution is, however, undesirable, since it would risk killing the motor of capital accumulation and entrepreneurship, which in turn would further reduce the economic growth rate. The right solution, argues Piketty, is a progressive tax on capital. This would make it possible to avoid the explosive concentration of wealth at the top of the distribution, while preserving competition and incentives for private accumulation of capital. An annual tax rate in the order of one percent on net wealth of one million euros, two percent on wealth between five and ten million, and perhaps an even higher rate for wealth above ten million, would contain the current trend for a concentration of capital. The problem lies in the practical implementation of such a tax. It cannot be implemented within the framework of the nation-state. Instead, it requires a high level of international cooperation. This may not be possible on a global scale, but it could perhaps be achieved within the framework of the EU, for example.

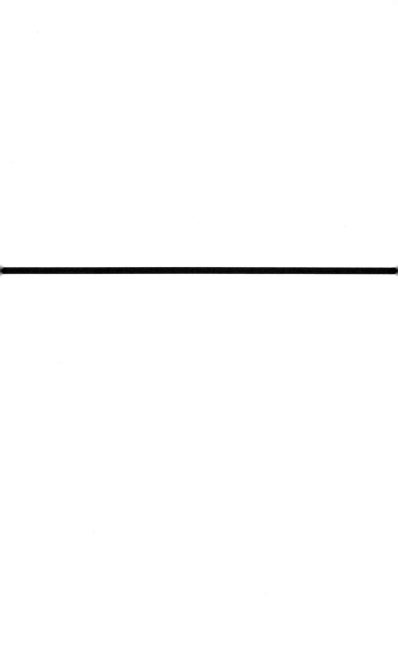

III

IS THOMAS PIKETTY
RIGHT?

Since its publication, Piketty's book has attracted both praise and criticism. Debate has raged about a number of elements of the book and it is, of course, impossible to comment on everything that has been said and written. Three areas of discussion can be distinguished: 1) is the data correct; 2) is the theoretical framework correct; and 3) are the policy suggestions appropriate?

Concerning the first issue of whether the various data series give an accurate picture of the developments, this debate flared up when a journalist from the reputable *Financial Times* declared that Piketty had made errors in his calculations, and that these errors changed the conclusions in the book. There are many facets to this discussion, but in the final analysis I firmly believe that the criticism in the *Financial Times* does not make any dramatic difference to the trends illustrated by the diagrams in Piketty's book. My understanding is also that most academic economists who have debated this issue would also agree with this conclusion.

Yet one can question some of the language Piketty uses in describing some of the developments seen in the data. For example, Piketty describes the wealth inequality development as moving toward levels of the nineteenth century. Figure 21 in this book (10.6 in Piketty) suggests this conclusion is not obvious from the data. In Piketty's defense, it might be said that achieving a satisfactory measure of wealth concentration is difficult and that, particularly today, there are good grounds to believe that large fortunes do not appear in the data. This does not, however, change the fact it is hard to see a return to the levels of the nineteenth century in the data presented here.

To some extent, this debate illustrates a general problem in understanding historical data and their limitations. They are often incomplete (as Piketty repeatedly points out), forcing researchers to make various guesses about things that cannot be observed. These guesses are naturally not made lightly, and a great deal of effort is put into getting as close to a true picture as possible, using various sources and alternative calculations. What eventually comes out of this is hopefully, if not an exact figure, at least a true picture of the trend. The only way to handle such a situation is to be clear about the methods one has used and what assumptions have been made in getting to the particular picture one chooses to present. In that respect, Thomas Piketty meets the highest possible standard. He has documented everything in great detail and generously shares all data and figures on his web page so that anyone interested in delving deeper into the facts can do so.

The second main area of debate has concerned Piketty's theoretical framework. Well-formulated criticism has for example come from Per Krusell at Stockholm University and Tony Smith at Yale. They focus on the relationship Piketty calls the *second fundamental law of capitalism*, which states the capital/income ratio over time converges with the saving rate divided by the growth rate, such that $\beta = K/Y = s/g$. Based on this, Piketty considers what happens to β when the growth rate goes down but the rate of saving remains constant. However, his reasoning, they argue, results in implausible conclusions when the growth rate heads towards zero. In that case, all income would ultimately go toward simply maintaining the stock of capital, which is, of course, not a likely outcome. It is much more plausible that saving goes down when growth falls, and in this case the effect on β is due to the relative fall in s and g. (For a more detailed account, see Per Krusell and Tony Smith's article "Is Piketty's Second Law of Capitalism Fundamental?")

As I see it, this debate is to a large extent about how literally to take the model. In several places in the book, Piketty is clear that savings are likely to go down as capital is accumulated, but more importantly he is also clear about not intending to formulate a theory of savings or growth. These depend on a host of factors and there does not appear to be any generally applicable relationship. Nevertheless, he believed the expression s/g explains the observable movements in the capital/income ratio, both between countries and over time. If, however, the expression is meant not as a general law, but as a relationship that captures historic fluctuations, it can understandably seem a little inappropriate to call it a "fundamental law."

Another important debate relates to the long-term validity of the relationship $r > g$, i.e., the return on capital over the long run is greater than growth over the long run. Several technical arguments can be put forward, but these hardly furnish us with any answers. Piketty no doubt took the view the issue cannot be resolved conclusively in a mathematical model. What he did in the book is to show, over much of our history, r has been significantly higher than g, and the key factors driving the change in this relationship during the twentieth century were the world wars and a number of other capital shocks. Against this background, he suggested, it is not unreasonable to expect $r > g$ will once again be true in the future and this, in turn, is likely to have certain effects on the income and wealth distribution.

As a reader, it is of course difficult to say what conclusions one should draw from this assertion, beyond the fact that the scenario painted by Piketty is a distinct possibility. It may be worth pointing out that the scenario of the relationship between r and g as posited in the book has not yet happened. Over the period 1950–2012, $g > r$ and it is only in the period 2012–2050 that this is expected to be reversed.

Finally, much has been said about the realism, or rather the lack of realism, in Piketty's proposal for a progressive wealth tax. Some of this debate is peculiar—Piketty was clear that he saw it as unrealistic, but he wanted to present the alternative in order to illustrate its virtues in principle. Personally, I feel it is very difficult to assess the consequences of the proposal when it is couched in such general terms. It seems reasonable to believe, in practice, a great deal rests on the type of capital that is taxed and exactly how it is done. The call for greater international cooperation when it comes to issues such as tax planning seems entirely right to me, however. It is not sustainable for individual countries to base future taxation on the principle of taxing what cannot be moved across borders—at least not if they want to retain the freedom for both capital and people to move across borders.

Why is the question of distribution important?

Putting aside Piketty's book, why is the question of distribution so important? For most people, it is a question of fairness. The fairness argument may, however, result in differing opinions on what the distribution should be and what (if anything) should be changed about it. Some place a strong emphasis on equal outcomes and believe, based on this notion, greater equality is important, irrespective of why the inequalities arise. Others believe inequalities, no matter how great they may be, are not only acceptable but fair; given everyone has had the same opportunities. The way the inequalities have arisen is crucial in determining what should or should not be done about them. This leads in turn to further discussions about what it means in practice, and how far we should go in trying to create the same opportunities for everyone.

In addition to these questions of fairness, one can see the distribution issue as critical for the way society functions. Following this discourse, it is possible to differentiate two channels via which distribution issues play a role: one economic and one political.

Along the economic channel, a person's decisions on education, investments, work, and so on are determined not only by the resources the person has available, but also by the expectations of what these decisions might lead to. In some societies, for example, education is expensive, which excludes those who cannot afford it. There may, however, be a consensus in society that education should be provided for free. Such redistribution increases the equality of opportunity between individuals. But it is not just resources that determine what decisions are taken.

In Piketty's book, Rastignac's dilemma is used in several places to illustrate the obvious negatives of a society in which the prospects offered by education and hard work are set against the option of inheriting or marrying into wealth (often with the conclusion that inheritance and marriage deliver much more than work and education). In a more modern Swedish context, it is not difficult to imagine alternative "dilemmas." As someone who grew up in Sweden in the 1970s and 1980s, I can testify it was not uncommon for young people at the time to question the economic rationale of getting an education and working hard, when alternative occupations appeared to pay just as well. The point is, questions of distribution are important in that they influence individual opportunities and incentives.

However, the distribution affects more than just an individual's decisions on investments, work, and education. Via the political channel, the distribution can also affect the way society's rules are shaped. One might reasonably fear a large concentration of wealth might affect the political process through lobbying and campaign contributions. In the worst case, such an effect could change the rules in a way that favors the current elite at the expense of free and fair competition, ultimately hurting how well the market economy functions. Finally, one can also imagine dissatisfaction with the distribution might result in a reaction against a policy that could potentially benefit everyone. An inability to share the benefits of globalization in a way that is considered reasonable could, for example, threaten the very policies on which globalization relies.

Photo credit: Paul Hansen

JESPER ROINE is an expert on wealth and income inequality, as well as one of the researchers who has contributed to the World Top Incomes Database upon which Piketty's research is based. He is an associate professor of Economics at SITE at the Stockholm School of Economics and has been published, extensively, on the topic of income and wealth inequality. Together with his colleague Daniel Waldenström at Uppsala University, he is responsible for the Swedish data on long-run income and wealth inequality used in Thomas Piketty's *Capital in the Twenty-First Century.*

Creditocracy
And the Case for Debt Refusal

Andrew Ross

ISBN 978-1-939293-38-1 PAPERBACK
ISBN 978-1-939293-39-8 E-BOOK
280 PAGES

In this forceful, eye-opening survey, Andrew Ross contends that we are in the cruel grip of a creditocracy—where the finance industry commandeers our elected governments and where the citizenry have to take out loans to meet their basic needs.

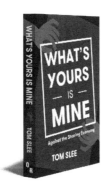

What's Yours Is Mine
Against the Sharing Economy

Tom Slee

ISBN 978-1-682190-22-7 PAPERBACK
ISBN 978-1-682190-23-4 E-BOOK
212 PAGES

In *What's Yours Is Mine*, technologist Tom Slee argues the so-called sharing economy extends harsh free-market practices into previously protected areas of our lives and presents the opportunity for a few people to make fortunes by pushing vulnerable individuals to take on unsustainable risk.